Award Winning 16th Century Inn
At the very heart of the Exmoor National Park

Set amidst high moorland, nestling beside the meandering river Exe in the picturesque village of Exford - Our 16th Century Coaching Inn has a long & proud tradition of welcoming travellers by foot, by hoof & by wheel.

Stay a while - With 28 individually designed rooms combining modern luxury with country charm. Spectacular riverside & moorland walks from our doorstep, stabling next door, we welcome families & dogs, the ideal location for your Exmoor adventure.

The true flavour of the moor - Enjoy a hearty meal in the relaxed atmosphere of a traditional Ale house, a delicious homemade cream tea served by the river or indulge in our celebrated Exmoor Sunday Carvery. Seasonal, local, fresh & distinctive are key elements to our la Carte menu rich in organic produce from surrounding farms and served in our elegant dining room.

A fireside sanctuary After a long day exploring the majestic moorland, relax in oak beamed bars serving a fine selection of real ales or on cold days a wee dram in our cosy lounge complete with a crackling fire. We boast one of the finest selections of single malts in the South West of England with over 200 whiskies for your approval.

With an ever changing season there is always a good reason to visit Exmoor.
We are open from daybreak to starry nights all year round....

- Morning Coffee • Bar Lunches
- Afternoon Teas and Evening Meals served daily throughout the year

THE MOORLAND MOUSIE TRUST

PROTECTING EXMOOR PONIES

The Moorland Mousie Trust and Exmoor Pony Centre are delighted to be continuing our work with Exmoor ponies. After a difficult time for everybody we are aware now more than ever how vital our outreach and wellbeing work is. The Charity has ensured the best care for all of our ponies and have relied upon the dedication and commitment of our staff and volunteers to assist in the survival of our charity.

In 2020/21 we took in over 20 ponies who needed our help and assisted many more through support schemes with pony owners.

The Moorland Mousie Trust is a leading organisation in the use of Exmoor ponies in environmental grazing schemes from 'rewilding' sites through to conservation grazing and land management sites. The Exmoor pony is an ever-popular choice, and we pride ourselves on the services, advice and guidance we offer to ensure the best care and management for these grazing ponies.

Our promotional work, which includes being a key partner in the Annual Exmoor Pony Festival, is ensuring a continued positive approach to the general awareness of the breed and in turn contributing to the positive impact on the purchasing of moorland foals in the Autumn.

We are always looking for more volunteers to help with the ponies, with fundraising and events. Please get in touch if you are interested in joining our friendly team.

Exmoor Pony Centre, Dulverton Somerset TA22 9QE
info@exmoorponycentre.org.uk
www.moorlandmousietrust.org.uk
01398 323093

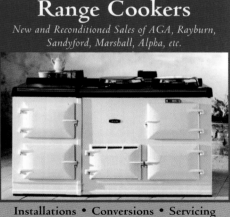

WOOLHANGER

Nestling amongst Exmoor's majestic hills
Woolhanger Manor invites you to share in
its glorious grandeur and spectacular scenery.
Let the mystical magic of Exmoor provide
a beautiful backdrop to your unique event.

As the centrepiece of a vast estate, Woolhanger
Manor and its historic Music Room offer peace,
privacy and picturesque views across the Exmoor
countryside and is a licensed wedding venue.

For a real taste of the unique and exclusive
Woolhanger please contact us to arrange
your private viewing.

Viewings by appointment only please

The Estate Office, Woolhanger Manor, Parracombe, Barnstaple EX31 4RF
Telephone 01598 763309   Email woolhangerestate@btconnect.com   www.woolhanger.com

7

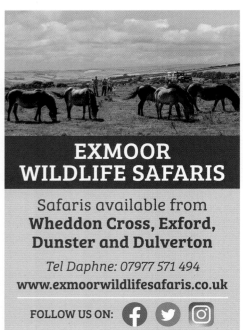

HALSGROVE

Publishing beautiful books for Somerset and beyond

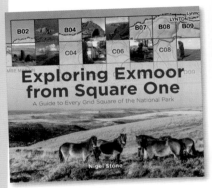

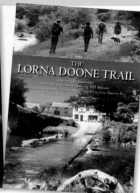

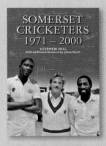
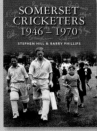

CONTENTS

FEATURES

MOOR LIFE

CHRISTMAS AT THE SOCIETY

CHRISTMAS CARD

Pixton Bridge/Selworthy, eco-packs of 10 cards and envelopes, two designs per pack.

£5 PER PACK

2022 WALL CALENDAR

A4 calendar of Exmoor Views, one page per month, eco-printed with card envelope.

2022 Calendar

June 2022
Bossington Hill View
©Madeline Taylor

£6 EACH

Available from our Dulverton shop or our online shop at www.exmoorsociety.com

THE EXMOOR SOCIETY

As we were going to press we learnt of the sad death of our President Sir Anthony Acland. A full obituary will appear in next year's *Review*.

The Exmoor Society works to protect and promote Exmoor's unique character. Founded in 1958 we are a membership organisation run by Trustees and work mainly through conferences and campaigning. We influence local and national policy through our statements, research and reports; we monitor planning and we have active outreach and awards programmes.

After an extraordinary year negotiating the uncertainties of Covid-19 the Society is back to 'business as usual'. The Resource Centre is open allowing access to our exhibitions and archive, our trustees are once again able to meet in person and preparations are well underway for our September AGM and the Spring Conference 2022. We have also redesigned this, our annual *Exmoor Review* and hope that you enjoy the new look.

Despite the challenges of social and often considerable geographical distance, the Society's work continued unabated and although operating from home, in many ways we were busier than ever. Below are just some highlights of 2020 and 2021, achievements that helped fulfil our charitable objective: to promote the conservation and protection of Exmoor National Park for the benefit of the public.

- Dealt with all the requirements of the Covid-19 pandemic whilst keeping the Society "open for business".

- Held a series of four live webinars in place of the annual Spring Conference.

- Advanced our Nature Recovery strategy with involvement in the Visualisation exercise by Exmoor National Park Authority (ENPA) and our promotion of the importance of "Nocturnal Exmoor".

- Continued our involvement in future farming schemes by supporting ENPA Test and Trials for Defra and our continued financial support for the Exmoor Hill Farming Network (EHFN).

- Welcomed people's enjoyment of the national park and developed a template for assessing sensitive sites for biodiversity, landscape quality, heritage and access.

- Appointed a new development co-ordinator to increase our presence on social media, corporate membership, and marketing.

- Pursued discussions on our commissioned "Towards a Register of Exmoor's Natural Capital" nationally and locally.

By no means complete, this list gives an idea of what we have accomplished – as The Year in Retrospect in this Review shows there is much more – all testament to the commitment and work of the officers, trustees and staff, for which many thanks. ◆

Rachel Thomas
August 2021

A BIGGER PICTURE

Rachel Thomas
Chairman, Exmoor Society

The Arts are a way of understanding change, of 'seeing' what a landscape is.

THE DOONE GLEN LYN

Our English National Parks have been in the glaring spotlight for the last three years – under examination to find out whether their role and purposes are fit for the 21st century.

Those landscapes designated National Parks over 74 years ago differed fundamentally from the first ones in the United States, where there were still monumental, pristine landscapes and people living in them were removed. Because of our history of a long settled, densely populated island we have no natural areas unaltered by human activity, but still there was a desire to set aside some of our finest, dramatic landscapes. Large and often open, tranquil with semi natural vegetation rich in wildlife and historic remains, the new parks were places where nature appeared dominant even though the land had been farmed, forested, mined and settled for thousands of years. They created opportunities for outside recreation for all to enjoy after the devastations of the Second World War. Today the situation is more complex, with our national parks facing crises both in the loss of biodiversity and adapting to climate change.

They remain in the spotlight while the government responds to the recommendations of the 2019 Landscapes (Glover) Review. Meanwhile, Brexit has occurred, the Agriculture Act passed and the Environment Bill almost, there are proposals to alter the Planning System and the impact of Covid-19 to work through. There is no need to wait, though, for government proposals in relation to Nature since these can be acted on immediately. Not least by the Exmoor National Park Authority which has been quick off the mark by introducing a vision for nature recovery to be achieved by 2030 with clear targets. "95% of existing wildlife areas being in favourable condition, 11,500 hectares of nature friendly farming areas", gives their flavour. Nature rich hubs are being proposed,

"...scenic beauty and the historic environment, may be unintentionally ignored and damaged; sacrificed to the urgency of addressing climate change and the loss of biodiversity."

'Doone Valley' by Alfred Robert Quinton c.1925. Watercolour, courtsey Salmon's

along the coast, in the central moorland block and in the smaller southern one that has fantastic views towards Dartmoor and where the area between seems unaltered since Saxon times. ENPA has also worked closely with the farming community through the Exmoor Hill Farming Network (ENFN) and others including ourselves, by taking part in Defra's Test and Trials for creating a new fully costed agri-environmental scheme called Exmoor's Ambition, based on Exmoor's Natural Capital Register, commissioned by the Society from Rural Focus.

There is a danger, however, that other important conservation assets and functions a national park provides, particularly its scenic beauty and the historic environment, may be unintentionally ignored and damaged; sacrificed to the urgency of addressing climate change and the loss of biodiversity. This loss would disregard the importance of the human influences that shape national parks and of human engagement in their continuing survival; engagement largely driven by the power of landscape and, in some important

respects, by its mediation through the arts.

The English word "landscape" came from the Dutch word "landschap" where 17th century Dutch painters focused on rural scenes with people engaged in rural pursuits. Phrases like "genius loci" and "spirit of place" were used later, meaning the essence of a place, or perhaps the qualities that inspire people by adding beauty, cheerfulness and hope to their lives. Today, "sense of place" or just "place" is the more popular term for the way our senses respond to the aesthetic and perceptual elements of landscape: sight, including colour, texture, pattern and form, sounds, smells, and touch.

> *"The Arts have an important role in getting people to look more deeply at landscapes, exploring changes or their absence."*

People's associations, their memories and experiences of different forms of recreation are also important.

Perhaps the most influential evocation of landscape's importance to people was that of the nineteenth century poets. In 1897 Wordsworth and Coleridge walked the Exmoor coast from the Quantocks to

'Lynmouth' by Spreat.
Private Collection

the Valley of Stones with Coleridge staying overnight in a farmhouse near Culbone feeling ill and awakening from a dream to compose *Kubla Khan*, short in length because he was interrupted by a person from Porlock. Painters followed and novelists and tourists.

The Arts have an important role in getting people to look more deeply at landscapes, exploring changes or their absence and articulating how beautiful landscapes affect them, especially today when emerging from very painful experiences such as the pandemic. The Exmoor Society with the backing and support of ENPA has therefore decided to commission a study from Professor Robin

McInnes called Art in Support of Improved Understanding of the Changing Character of Exmoor National Park. The proposal accepts that historical evidence, including artworks, old photographs, literature accounts and maps, provide a rich source of evidence about the nature, scale and rate of change over time and allows it to be better understood.

The research will use full colour art images covering the period from the 1770s to the present day. It will be based on Exmoor's nine different landscapes identified in the 2018 Landscape Character Assessment by ENPA, that was made with the full involvement with the Exmoor Society. The Assessment provides a tool to integrate the conservation of the natural world with the cultural landscape. The results of the study should help people to become more involved in wider landscape/environmental matters and lead to a series of activities including an art and photographic competition, discussion on future landscape change, the linking of ENPA Historic Environment Record to the Exmoor Society Archives and 'Then and Now' project, a landscape art trail and, not least, inspiring people to explore and enjoy the many ways landscape contributes to their general wellbeing.

David Hockney's 2012 exhibition in the Royal Academy reinforced the importance of landscape painting in a way that resonates with the present generation. People attended in their thousands to look at his pictures of trees and seasons ranging from a winter afternoon, through the slow incremental burst of spring, to the summer hedges thick with flowers, to autumn with its flaming colours. Hockney's use of new technology such as the iPad, and the sheer size of the pictures, captured the imagination and absorbed the viewer in the trees and hedgerows with paths to follow while passing through the woods and seeing seasonal changes.

A priority now in making National Parks fit for the 21st century, is to raise awareness of the crises ahead. At the same time to engage people positively in different ways, providing choices and for some this will be by using the power of landscape painting. Each generation has to explore Exmoor's changing landscape character for itself to discover its layers of meaning and deeper delights. ◆

As the Barle Turns (Clover Godsal)

Brendon Two Gates (ENPA)

CRYING THE MOOR

A Miscellany of Exmoor News

In the days when someone's naked voice was the best broadcaster of information, each spring the price for grazing on Exmoor that summer was proclaimed in neighbouring towns. After the summer came the announcement of the annual roundup of stock for sale in these towns. 'Crying the Moor' was the term used, with some writers now understanding that it referred to the first of these activities and others to the second, or possibly to both.

FARMING

WHAT IS THE ELMS?

Basic payments to farmers in England will be halved by 2024 and phased out completely by 2028. Government support will then be focused on the ELMS or the Environmental Land Management Schemes. There are some real opportunities now to move forward in ways that provide benefit to all, however, there is a distinct lack of detail. The process is being informed by a number of regional studies, including one on Exmoor. The Exmoor study has raised some serious concerns including, potential threats to important designated habitats in upland areas like Exmoor and potential barriers to farms being able to access ELMs funding. A national pilot is due to start later this year with further pilots in 2022. All businesses need time to plan, farming is no exception and the anxiety caused by this policy vacuum is palpable. 2024 will come very soon.

HOW FARE OUR BEEF AND SHEEP FARMERS?

Given that "Crying the Moor" refers to the historic process of communicating prices for grazing, each year I try to update readers of the Review with regard to the current concerns, financial and otherwise, that are affecting farming families on Exmoor. Previously I have reported on the ups and downs of the beef and sheep market. In summary, to paraphrase an old saying, "when it is good it is okay and when it is bad it is horrid." During 2020 the price for beef and lamb gradually strengthened. In part this was because of decreased supply (farmers had cut back their herds and flocks because of uncertainty around Brexit) and also increased demand. In lockdown consumers bought more beef and lamb and I think it is fair to say that home-grown meat features more heavily

in supermarkets supply chains than in the food service industry's supply chains (we were not eating out). The result was a 40p per kilo deadweight premium for beef and 80p per kilo deadweight for lamb (though at one stage in April this was closer to £2). As I write the beef price is holding up, but with new season lamb the lamb price plummeted £30-£35 per head in June though it is still up on the previous year. This lack of stability is not sustainable. Supplies of affordable good quality food are a social good.

Sean Beer

EXMOOR'S AMBITION TEST AND TRIAL, PRELIMINARY CONCLUSIONS

The Exmoor's Ambition ELM Test and Trial was led by Exmoor National Park, supported by the Exmoor Hill farm Network, and funded by DEFRA, with 26 farmers and landowners contributing. It tested the viability of a Natural Capital accounting model on Exmoor farms and woodlands and developed a set of

Exmoor Farmers Livestock Auction

potential payment options on the 'public money for public goods' basis whilst also defining local and national environmental priorities on Exmoor.

The move to a land management policy based on environmental expectation via Sustainable Farming Incentive (SFI), Environmental Land Management (ELM), Nature Recovery Networks and Landscape Recovery represents a huge change in approach and complexity which is why these concepts needed testing.

Although most farmers embraced the concept of natural capital to measure the assets on their farms when drawing up land management plans, the terminology is still misunderstood. Mapping is absolutely fundamental to identifying opportunities but has to broadly follow national priorities whilst recognising specific local priorities.

Adviser support at different levels will probably be the key to full engagement and payment levels may well be the ultimate determining factor for success. The income foregone approach for calculating payment levels is unlikely to offer enough to cover the activities required and, although payment for environmental outcomes was embraced by many, it was felt that ELM payments would need to be significantly higher than at present to cover fixed costs as well as cost of delivery. Underfunding could lead to reductions in land management with many unforeseen consequences for Exmoor.

In an era of change where risks and opportunities become ever greater our thanks must go to all those contributing to this work and their enthusiasm in facilitating a future for Exmoor that will be to the benefit of all. The full report can be found on the ENPA website.

Robin Milton

Badgworthy Wood (Brian Pearce)

WOODS

THE 30-YEAR WOODLAND STRATEGY FOR EXMOOR NATIONAL PARK

Exmoor's woodland is special: deeply incised wooded valleys, wild ancient coastal woodlands, verdant temperate rainforest, designed landscapes of trees and woods, rare and veteran trees, old estate mixed woodlands and more recent highly productive conifer plantations. 14% or 9500 ha of Exmoor is now woodland providing benefits for people, nature, and the economy. We would like to ensure our existing woodlands continue to do this but also ensure that they provide a deeper and wider range of benefits through increased areas under management, intervention and protection so that people connect with woodlands in a meaningful way.

We currently import more timber than any other country except China. This demand for imported timber from regions with little regulation or control helps drive environmental damage and social problems overseas. We would like to see more of our own high- quality timber harvested in genuinely sustainable ways from Exmoor's woodlands.

Our trees and woods are at greater risk than ever before. Diseases and pests are already having a dramatic and devastating impact. We are likely to lose 95% of the estimated 600,000 ash trees on Exmoor, many other pests and diseases threaten our trees and woods.

At 14% Exmoor's woodland cover is slightly higher than the national average, but we believe we can increase this to 17% – 19%, or 12-13,000 ha, over the 30-year life of the Woodland Strategy, with a creation rate of around 100 ha/year. This would be in-line with a national woodland creation target of 30,000 ha/year – more than double the area of new woodland planted in 2018. We would like to go well beyond this. We will work with communities and our partners to explore opportunities to increase tree and woodland cover and in a way which enhances and respects the special qualities of the National Park. We will explore innovative techniques to blend trees and farming on a more expansive scale, to blur the edges between woodland and open habitats, to relieve pressures preventing natural tree regeneration and connect and restore habitats, landscapes and people in new and exciting ways.

This strategy will help to guide these ambitions and support our shared visions for landscape, nature, farming and heritage.

Graeme McVittie

HOUSING

The National Park Authority have appointed a Rural Housing enabler, Nic Kemp, for the Somerset part of Exmoor. She has worked with the eight parishes Affordable Housing Working Group which has been considering seven potential sites for the development of local affordable housing. Of these two sites in Cutcombe and one in Exford received clear support and there was likely support for sites in Luxborough and Timberscombe.

Nic Kemp has also been upgrading Homefinder – the register that allows those in housing need to bid on available properties. She is working with Exmoor Young Voices on the self-build project and there are currently 13 individuals on the Self-Build Register who fulfil the local connection criterion. In addition, she is relaunching the Exmoor Rural Housing Network with an annual meeting planned in October.

The Housing Needs Surveys, based on six surveys carried out since 2016, show that there are 49 households currently in affordable housing need on Exmoor.

Between 2017 and 2020 there have been 4 permissions for affordable housing and 23 completions.

CONSERVATION

MEADOW-MAKERS GROUP

Earlier this year, an online platform was launched to form a new 'meadow-makers' group on Exmoor. Organised by the conservation group Moor Meadows, this forum aims to bring people together to improve the number of wildflowers within the national park. It also enables members to share information and advice on how to create wildflower meadows as well as being kept up to date with news and events from across the group. With only 2% of the country's grassland habitats rich in wildflowers, every field, paddock, churchyard, road verge and garden that can be converted to a well-managed meadow is a vital space for wildlife.

Anyone on Exmoor who is keen to take part in this scheme can join free by visiting http://forum.moremeadows.org.uk

FIRST BABY BEAVER TO BE BORN ON EXMOOR FOR 400 YEARS

The first 'kit' has been born to the pair of beavers released onto the Holnicote Estate back in January 2020. During the recent Nocturnal Exmoor webinars, estate ranger Jack

Siviter explained what brilliant ecosystem engineers beavers are and how they are re-forming Exmoor's landscape. "Having the beavers here helps us to manage the water in a more natural way. The ponds created behind the dams become living structures and have multiple benefits including regeneration of plants, creation of spawning grounds alongside carbon capture".

WORKING TOWARDS A PLASTIC FREE EXMOOR

Every day 8 million pieces of plastic pollution enters our oceans. Tackling this problem head on is marine conservation charity Surfers Against Sewage, who have launched a Plastic Free Communities campaign to encourage people across the UK to reduce their use of single-use plastic. So far 802 communities have signed up with 156 already certified including Porlock Vale, Minehead and Watchet. Exmoor National Park Authority have also pledged to become plastic free and are currently working towards their accreditation.

Alongside communities, businesses are encouraged to become Plastic Free Champions. To achieve this status, they need to find innovative ways to remove single use plastic alongside promoting the campaign to their network. Businesses across Exmoor have stepped up to this challenge including The Exmoor Tea Company, the Kind Kitchen, and the *Exmoor Magazine*.

For more information, visit http://plasticfree.org.uk/

CREATION OF A DARK SKY DISCOVERY HUB

New for 2021 is the creation of a Dark Sky Discovery Hub on Exmoor. Exford Bridge tearooms have collaborated with local business, Wild About Exmoor, to create a centre for information and events, all focused on the dark skies of Exmoor. The hub's aim is to inspire people to make the most of the dark by hosting astronomical events as well as providing information about current meteor shows, visible planets and where to find them and phases of the moon. To learn more or to book events visit: https://wildaboutexmoor.com/exmoor-dark-skies-discovery-hub/. ◆

Laura Yiend

(Laurence Liddy)

NOCTURNAL EXMOOR

This May, the Exmoor Society held a series of four webinars – their theme was 'Life in the Dark'

'THE DARKNESS REVEALED' *Nigel Hester*

An Exmoor farmer once told me that the time of day he liked best was when night fell at the end of the day and he shut the farmhouse door. Yes, there was the satisfaction of finishing a day's work, but there was also the thought that wildlife could now reclaim the world. During the day the farmyard was dominated by human activity: the hubbub of tractors and quad bikes, the bark of working dogs, the shouts moving livestock, the noise of cattle, sheep, horses and poultry. Night was different, it was the time of bats, mice, voles, rabbits, foxes, deer and, of course, owls. The farmer said that although he couldn't see it, he knew it was there – and that he was honoured to share his farm with all this wildlife.

In the Spring of 2020, the idea for a project based on the dark and the night was put forward by the Society's Trustees. Its ambition was to celebrate the abundance of wildlife associated with the night on Exmoor and to assess the pressures and threats to this oft-hidden fauna.

Our regular Spring Conference was cancelled by Covid last year, so this May we replaced it with a series of four webinars, Nocturnal Exmoor. Rather than concentrate just on wildlife, the theme of the night sky and darkness was broadened to encompass its effect on people's lives, the creative arts and culture and a celebration of the night sky itself.

The impact of light on the lives of mammals and insects was the subject of the first webinar's keynote talk by Prof Fiona Mathews. Dr Elizabeth Bradshaw followed with an introduction to the fifteen species of bats that live within Exmoor. Finally, Jack Siviter, the National Trust's Riverland's Ranger, gave a glimpse into the night lives of the two pairs of beavers reintroduced to the Holnicote Estate in January 2020, after a 400-year absence from Exmoor and their remarkable eco-system engineering.

Focussing on the rhythms of night and day, the second webinar began with the author Tim Dee tracing the long, migratory journey of three iconic bird species from South Africa to Horner

> *"Night was different, it was the time of bats, mice, voles, rabbits, foxes, deer and, of course, owls."*

Wood, Exmoor. The next speaker was Holly Purdey, who runs Horner Farm in the Porlock Vale with her husband Mark. She described how night affects their working lives, the natural behaviour of their livestock and the presence of nocturnal wildlife on the farm. She has learnt that sheep and cattle are troubled when they are disturbed at night, particularly when calving or lambing, so when she checks her stock Holly uses a head torch rather than switching on the bright barn lights. The dark hours bring peace and tranquility but, as Holly vividly described, night work also takes a toll on farmers. She also discussed the joy that nightfall brings after a busy working day – the chance to see friends and family, a time to relax and unwind.

The third webinar opened with a fascinating talk by conservation architect Giles Quarme on the historical impact of night and artificial light on Exmoor lives. Susan Derges, a photographic artist living and working in Devon followed with a wonderfully illustrated talk. Her acclaimed work is held in a number of important museums around the world, including the Metropolitan Museum in NY and the Victoria & Albert Museum in London. Susan has lived on Dartmoor for the last 30 years and uses light sensitive paper, sometimes coloured, to create images of the night sky, watery environments and natural vegetation. The whole landscape, in effect, is her photographic darkroom. Her work using rivers, especially the Taw, has resulted in exquisite images reflecting the flow and eddy of the water with stark outlines of overhanging shrubs and trees. It often resonates with Japan, where she lived for a period.

The final speaker was Victoria Eveleigh, or Tortie as she is better known on Exmoor. Author of the successful children's book *Midnight on Lundy*,

Tortie lives and farms with her husband, Chris, at West Ilkerton. She prefers to write during the small hours when interruptions are kept to a minimum and she can enter 'the zone'. She reminded us how enchanting night-time can be for children – a sleepover at a

"... if you venture out into the farmyard at midnight you will hear the animals talking!"

different house or a bonfire with toasted marshmallows! And how, on the night before Christmas at their farm, the magic is there whatever your age and it is said that if you venture out into the farmyard at midnight you will hear the animals talking!

The last webinar focussed on the night sky. The keynote speaker was Jo Richardson who represents the South West as one of 10 UK Space Ambassadors. Jo runs Space Detectives that introduces space and astronomy to children and adults alike. She is a Fellow of the Royal Astronomical Society and no stranger to Exmoor, having been involved in the events celebrating Exmoor National Park's Dark Sky Reserve. Jo brought to life the wonders of the Milky Way, visible from most of Exmoor but warned that light pollution and the more recent threat from the vast array of satellites being placed in orbit will seriously reduce our ability to see and study the night sky. Katrina Munro, the Economy Project Officer for ENPA, followed with a presentation on Exmoor's Dark Sky Reserve. Exmoor was declared to be Europe's first Dark Sky Reserve in 2011 and to celebrate the 10th anniversary, there will be a Dark Skies

Festival from 22nd October until 7th November.

Despite glitches and gremlins the webinars were greatly enjoyed and they are available on the Society's website and YouTube. The one talk that is missing is that of Rob Wilson-North, ENPA's head of Conservation & Access, whose connection failed although his pen didn't: we are fortunate to have an article in this Review to tell the story of the historical perception of Exmoor at night.

We are very grateful to Anne Parham, the Society Administrator, for hosting them and for all her hard work behind the scenes. ◆

Blagdon Cross with Star Trails (Adrian Cubitt)

LIGHTS OFF!

Artificial light is having a devastating impact on nocturnal mammals. *Professor Fiona Mathews*

Artificial light at night is a very recent human invention. It is so ubiquitous that it is easy to forget that when the streetlighting was introduced, the lamps were only to be lit on moonless nights. In evolutionary time-scales, illumination of the night sky has happened in the blink of an eye. Bats have been flying for around 50 million years, and moths pre-dated them by at least 150 million years. In contrast, Pall Mall, the first public street to be lit with gas lamps, was illuminated in 1807, and the first electric street lights were switched on in Paris in 1878.

> *"… the night sky has been lit up to such an extent that most people in industrial countries see nothing but the brightest of stars, this is by no means a 'normal' environment for nocturnal animals."*

We humans are very highly dependent on colour vision, and so most of our activities naturally coincide with daylight. Lighting designers therefore often use wavelengths of light that give us a similar colour perception to our daytime experience. This is partly why there has been a move away from older lighting types such as mercury vapour (white) and low-pressure sodium (deep orange) lights.

However, our perspective is not representative of the animal kingdom. Over 60% of terrestrial mammal species, 90% of amphibians and 50% of insects are nocturnal; and many others are active primarily at dawn and dusk. These animals have optimized their vision for low levels of light, and also make greater use of their other senses. They are also critical to our ecosystems. For example, about a third of all terrestrial mammal species are bats that hoover up countless insects every night. Moths are important pollinators and their caterpillars are key prey for birds and other species. They have evolved to be active at night, often to avoid predation, and the sudden introduction of light is as disruptive to them as the energy crisis of the 1970s was to humans: remember when the lights went out how we fumbled for candles?

My colleague Jens Rydell carried out some remarkable work investigating the impacts of illuminating churches at night in Sweden. He showed that it had catastrophic effects on the bats roosting in church roofs. Of sites occupied by breeding long-eared bats in the 1980s when the churches were unlit, fewer than 20% of churches with exterior lighting still had their bats in 2016, compared with 70% of those that remained unlit.

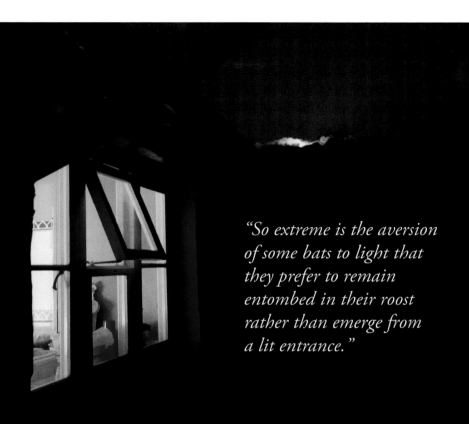

> "So extreme is the aversion of some bats to light that they prefer to remain entombed in their roost rather than emerge from a lit entrance."

(Nigel Hester)

So extreme is the aversion of some bats to light that they prefer to remain entombed in their roost rather than emerge from a lit entrance: this has been shown for Natterer's bats in England, and as a consequence Natural England no longer permit lights to be used as a means of 'moving bats on' before construction work starts in bat occupied buildings.

My research group has also shown that lighting is one of the strongest factors determining how rare greater horseshoe bats – some of which are found in Exmoor – move around the landscape. Lights therefore not only affect where bats can live, but also where they can forage. You might find this a surprise if you have ever seen bats hunting insects around a streetlight. However, whilst it is true that species that naturally emerge very early from their roosts are happy enough to make use of this concentrated food supply, most of our rare bats are woodland- and cave-dwelling species and extremely light-shy.

The attraction of insects to lights, "as moths to a flame", is itself a problem. Many species are attracted over extremely long-distances, and once caught in the cone of light remain trapped there until the light is turned off or they die of exhaustion. The result is that the local landscape is denuded of the pollination services and food resources that these insects provide. In addition, any moth flying around a light is not doing what moths need to be doing – namely making more moths. In some species, males are particularly strongly attracted, ignoring the egg-laden females who are flying closer to the ground, ready to mate and deposit their eggs.

Even birds are not immune from the effects of night lighting. Whilst many species are diurnal, many migrate under the cover of darkness, and some seabirds, such as manx shearwaters and storm petrels, only come ashore to feed their chicks at night. Coastal lighting, and lighting of oil rigs and cruise liners can cause massive disruption to these species, disorientating birds that are unable to use their normal celestial compass (navigating by the stars).

What can we do about all this? Although lighting is one of the most pervasive and rapidly increasing environmental pollutants, we can all take action to reverse the trend. We can draw our curtains at night to avoid interior light spilling into the environment. We can think carefully about how we deploy exterior lighting and assess whether the light is needed at all. Although it may seem counter-intuitive, our night vision is pretty good and is actually disrupted by the presence of lighting. Where lighting is needed keep it in places where it is useful and do not allow it to spill out into the wider environment. Countless security lights illuminate not only the building of interest, but also the garden of the house next door and the field beyond.

Good lighting design can be a help. Look for lights that are shielded so that light is focused to where it is needed.

"Although lighting is one of the most pervasive and rapidly increasing environmental pollutants, we can all take action to reverse the trend."

Globes, lanterns and bollard lighting are often particularly poor in this regard. We can reduce the amount of light we use not only by switching lights off (do you really need your porch light to be on at 3am?) but by reducing their intensity. Many exterior lights are crazily over-powered, and there is very little regulatory control. We can also avoid white and blue-white lights, which seem to have the largest ecological impact, and lights reflecting off water or white walls. Finally, we can encourage our local councils and communities to think about wildlife when lighting is installed. ◆

THINK!

- Do you really need it?
- Draw your curtains
- Downlighters not uplighters
- Warm light not blue or white
- Focus light to just where it needs to be
- Switch lights off when they aren't needed

Let's keep Exmoor's dark skies dark!

DARKNESS AND LIGHT

Electricity and light pollution have blurred the division between night and day. We no longer fear the dark nor are we bound by it. Conservation Architect *Giles Quarme*, illuminates the hardship of rural life in the dark ages.

Light has always been a symbol for the move out of ignorance into the light of knowledge. As long as we can manufacture and control light, then we are no longer bound by the seasons, or forced to work from sunrise to sunset.

Deborah Swift,
The Tallow Chandler[1]

My mother bought 6 Lanehead, at Porlock Weir in 1959. She knocked the two end cottages together. She had to fight the County Council, which had 'condemned' the properties and was within two weeks of demolishing them. They had stone floors, low ceilings and no indoor sanitation or electricity and only open

A pre-1914 Dulverton shop selling lamps

fires on the ground floor. The cottages were served by outside earth closets, two together for the adults and a row of six for the children. With no electricity, and because she only had one tilly lamp to light the ground floor, we used torches when going upstairs to bed.

It seemed romantic, but before electricity life in Exmoor cottages was dark and cold. Open fires provided heating, light and cooking.

Cottages tended to have only two rooms on the ground floor, one for the family and the other was the Parlour which was reserved for special occasions. The upstairs bedrooms were without fireplaces and, of course, unlit. The rich with their silver candlesticks were better served. They had beeswax candles, but these were very expensive. According to the book of *Country House Lighting*[2]:

"It seemed romantic, but before electricity life in Exmoor cottages was dark and cold. Open fires provided heating, light and cooking."

the cost of wax candles ensured that few were burnt when the family were on their own. It is said, for instance, that during the winter of 1756 at Audley End, (a mansion twice the size of Dunster Castle), only about 12 candles were burnt each night.

For middle and working classes, tallow candles, consisting of a wick in animal fat, were the norm. They were extremely smelly. In the mid-19th century, they were gradually replaced by spermaceti (whale blubber) and paraffin wax, followed by gas, which was twelve times as bright as a candle, and eventually electricity.

But even tallow candles were beyond the resources of the poor, who depended on rush lights. In 1904 Gertrude Jekyll described how these worked:

An old cottage friend told me all about it, and though she was 90 years of age, yet, when next I went to see her, she had gone out and found some rushes to show me how it was done. You peels away the rind from the peth, leaving only a little strip and when the rushes is dry you dip em through the grease keeping em well under and my mother always laid hers to dry in a bit of hollow bark. Mutton fats the best: it dries hardest.

In cottages the main source of light was the open fireplace and so fuel for these was a constant need. Cottagers had no rights to cut down trees on anyone's land, but often their employers would allow them to collect dead wood. The other fuel was turf. As Rob Wilson-North explains this was cut throughout the moor. But turf, even when well dried, burns poorly and issues little heat and virtually no light. It was very much the poor man's fuel.

Rushlight

Peat Cutting on Brendon Common, courtesy of Michael Berry

Coal was brought from Wales across the Bristol Channel to Porlock Weir and other small ports with the same boats returning with lime and oak pit props. The Kiln at Porlock Weir was built over lime kilns, which still exist. The adjoining Weybridge Cottage was once a small single cell office building with a coal weighbridge, which survived until the late 1960s. This would be burnt in coal ranges that gradually replaced both the open fires and the bread ovens so characteristic of Exmoor cottages.

Our image of the past is often perceived through the rose-tinted glasses of Alfred Robert Quinton's chocolate box watercolours but as well as being dark, Exmoor life was dangerous. The *North Devon Journal* provides us with an interesting picture of contemporary behaviour and mores. It is like a sourcebook for a Dickens novel, which ranges from the humorous, such as in 1841, William Gabriel, a Barnstaple beadle, is fined 5/- for being so drunk that he had to be taken to the police station in a wheelbarrow, to the tragic case of George Thomas, aged 9,

"Darkness was everywhere associated with poverty, crime and prostitution."

transported to Australia for the theft of just under £2 in 1837. In the same year Anne Locke, a pauper woman in Pilton died of starvation and the Inquiry jury blamed the Poor Law Officers for 'heartlessness'. But poverty and hunger persisted: in 1867 in Barnstaple, 3,000 people rioted over food prices and it took the Volunteer Rifles and 200 Special Constables to pacify the town. Darkness was everywhere associated with poverty, crime and prostitution. In 1856, the Journal reckons that out of the 4800 females in Barnstaple there were three hunderd prostitutes. It was this fear of the dark and its relationship to poverty that was behind the effort to bring streetlights to Barnstaple in the 1820s.

Conditions around Porlock began to improve in the 1820s when the Aclands set about developing their estate, starting with their house at Holincote. Thatch, normally associated with vernacular architecture, is here an image of sophistication. Concurrent with its construction were the "improvements" to the cottages of Selworthy that transformed it into a picturesque village in the late 1820s. Notably, however, this was done for old retainers, not local villagers. But the Aclands, as benevolent landlords, also ensured that their villages were well maintained, as Luccombe and Bossington bear witness. These improvements were limited though and until recently cottages lacked most essential amenities. The Mass Observation Unit provided an account of life in Luccombe in 1948:

There are baths in the two new council houses with cold taps and drains. Mrs Howard uses hers for two children who have a weekly tub from water heated in the copper. The next-door bath is not used as they only have kettles for water heating. One villager has a bath in her kitchen, but without outlet and is not used. Another has a hip bath which is not used either. None of the cottages has a water heating system and so far as can be ascertained, it is the usual and perhaps universal practice in the village to have a strip-wash in a basin.

Alfred Robert Quinton, Painting of Bossington 1912. *An Endless View*

In the mid-1960s the National Trust tenants, mostly pensioners, who lived in the Holnicote estate cottages still only had earth closets at the bottom of their gardens and this was probably also when electricity was installed.

It is only fifty years, but with the coming of light and heat, of gas and electricity to Exmoor's remote villages and cottages, how things have changed. As Martin Pawley poignantly puts it:

> Remaining country cottages in most parts of Britain have become prized as country homes. One in Oxfordshire boasts a Jaguar, where 60 years before a previous tenant and his family committed suicide as a result of hunger. ◆

[1] Deborah Swift, The Tallow Chandler, http://the-history-girls.blogspot.com/2018/01/trade-in-17th-century-tallow-chandler.html

[2] Country House Lighting, Temple and Newsam Studies No. 4: Trustees of the Victoria and Albert Museum

[3] Martin Pawley, Architecture versus Housing, Littlehampton Book Services, 1971

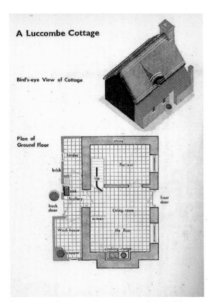

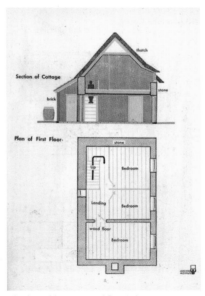

Diagram of Luccombe cottage, (Mass Observation Archive, University of Sussex)

WOLF MOON OVER EXMOOR*

As I drove through the darkening night,
I felt a distant lupine aching.
Alone on the road, alone at home
Travelling the ancient Pilgrim's Way
Past Raleigh's Cross to the steep hill brow

Without warning, by creeping stealth it
Startled
Showed Somerset's patchwork perfection
Spread below its bright luminescence.

This giant orb of polarized light
From the ancient Farmer's Almanac
Held a mirror to my inner wolf:
I bayed out emotions unrestrained,
Craving company, finding fury
The rapacious hunger of solitude
Crystalised in plain moonlit relief

At the very peak of my descent
I became wolfish, savage and hungry;
Starved of what I needed, I howled aloud.

Then, quietly, yet ever watchful
The wolf disappeared.
Hidden by the lucent woodlands

Exmoor moonlight shone like a beacon,
Starkly reflecting the reminder
That craving is the cry of survival

*The January full moon is referred to as the Wolf Moon as it was the time when wolves were at their most savage: starved over the lean winter months and their howling at the wolf moon signalled a dangerous hunger that needed to be fed.

Dora Allen, winner of the Exmoor Society Poetry Competition

Horner Wood (Pete Rae)

OUT OF AFRICA, INTO HORNER

The miracle that brings wood warblers, redstarts and pied flycatchers to Horner Wood each spring. *Tim Dee*

An Exmoor morning in late April in the hanging oak woods at Horner. I follow Boy's Path through the trees around a contour of the slopes of Dunkery. There is a wood warbler singing from the crown of a fresh green oak. Its song tumbles from it, a silver thread being pulled from a trembling body. It is beautiful to hear. And it wasn't in the wood yesterday when I took the same path. I saw then the other two members of what I think of as the holy trinity of spring migrant birds at Horner. Every redstart, pied flycatcher, and now, wood warbler in the wood will have crossed the Sahara from their wintering places in Africa. Every one of them, none weighing more than 10 grammes, is already a veteran and a survivor. Last autumn, each traversed the sand heading south to reach those wintering places. All three of these waif-like birds, seemingly so delicate, fly at night.

I've been to the desert in Chad looking for the trinity in places other than their spring breeding grounds on Exmoor. It is terrifying and the wood warbler at Horner crossed it twice in the last eight or nine months. The Sahara runs to 12 million square km (the size of the USA); it is 1000-1500km from north to south; there is precious little vegetation; the air temperature is often 40 degrees Celsius, the sand temperature 70 degrees and it is getting tougher. The desert is expanding north and south thanks to human influences and the green cycle of the Sahara: as the world climate pulses and flexes over many thousands of years this cycle means that softer, wetter and greener epochs alternate, as they are now, with the heat of the deep baked hard desert.

> *"To any bird the Sahara is a formidable barrier and yet 5000 million individuals of 186 land bird species cross it twice every year."*

To any bird the Sahara is a formidable barrier and yet 5000 million individuals of 186 land bird species cross it twice every year. There are concentrations of these birds at the slightly easier crossing places, on the desert's western and eastern edges where there is coastal scrub and the wetness of the Nile Valley to offer some succour, but many birds migrate across its broad centre. And indeed, migration makes sense – it is adaptive; they do it because of the opportunities it brings them. Wood warblers couldn't survive a winter at Horner but the goodness of springtime on Exmoor makes the risks of migration worthwhile.

The wood warbler at Horner may well have hatched in the wood the year before I heard it sing. Amazingly – I must ration myself with this word, almost everything about migration can literally *amaze* us – just a few weeks out of its egg and knowing only a hillside of green trees, it will have left and moved south on its own and mostly at night. It doesn't know where it must go or where it will end up: young birds seemingly have little more than an innate directional urge to head south. If it makes it out of Europe and across the Mediterranean it will fly on over the western Sahara until it comes to a stop on the south side of the desert, its winter home. If it is a good place and the bird survives the next six months it will

Wood warbler (Richard Bennett)

Pied flycatcher (Ben Andrew)

turn around (how it knows to do this is still barely understood – does it discern the barely discernible, the tiny variations in day length at the equator?) Again at night and again alone, it will journey north, potentially all the way back to the same trees on the hillside at Horner.

To cross the Sahara many birds double their body weight. They lay down fat around the keel of their breastbone. Coming north, Exmoor's wood warblers fatten up below the Sahara in west Africa; on their way south, Horner's pied flycatchers fatten up in western Iberia, they are then able to fly across the whole desert in one flight. Small birds fly at roughly 35km per hour – they need 72 hours for the desert alone. In the daytime some descend to crouch motionless in the shade of rocks.

The climate crisis is messing with the birds on their journeys but also at either end of their flights. Pied flycatchers are now arriving on Exmoor out of

synchrony with the peak abundance of caterpillars they feed on. Wood warblers have adapted to take other insects in England but are suffering because their woodland habitat in West Africa is being destroyed for agriculture. The desert should be punishment enough for these birds but it seems that we are hurrying them towards oblivion.

Even when life goes well, to make these journeys the birds need the equivalent of a map, a compass, a calendar, and a clock. And a memory. None of them have brains bigger than a pea. It is little wonder that many early naturalists concocted theories

"He held on to a widespread belief that the birds hibernated in the mud at the bottom of ponds."

to explain what happens to the birds they watched in the European summer after they left those skies. Gilbert White was painstakingly accurate in his studies yet couldn't quite believe that the swallows he loved around him every Hampshire summer left the county and the country and went perhaps as far away as the Cape of Good Hope. He held on to a widespread belief that the birds hibernated in the mud at the bottom of ponds.

Migration is more believable, even explicable, when you can see it. There are diurnal as well as nocturnal migrants. Crows, pipits, wagtails, larks, finches, tits, Gilbert White's swallows and other hirundines fly by day. Warblers, thrushes, flycatchers, and chats migrate by night. While Gilbert held on to his hibernation fantasy, his brother John saw swallows crossing the Straits of Gibraltar and knew that they left Hampshire. Longer distance migrants are more likely to be night flyers – though swallows are an exception to this. When you see night migrants arriving in the daytime, say in the early spring on the northern shore of the Mediterranean, you are most likely looking at birds that set off from North Africa at sunset the day before on a journey that took them more than twelve hours. The mind, forgives Gilbert White and boggles.

Why do the night flyers travel in the dark? It is energy, time and risk saving. There is more time for feeding during the day; lower temperatures prevent overheating and dehydration; humidity, which is higher at night, further reduces the risk of dehydration. Energy demands are lower as it is easier to fly in cool, dense night air; wind speeds are lower and so is the risk of predation. The birds lose sleep, but they are adapted to this at migration times – some sleep in the day,

Redstart (Ben Andrew)

with power naps when one half of the brain sleeps at a time (though how bar-tailed godwits go without sleep for up to ten days of non-stop flight from Alaska to New Zealand is still not understood).

They set off in the hours after sunset when their colour vision goes and they fly high; most at 1000–3000 metres, although new research has shown that great reed warblers climb to 5000 metres. How they navigate remains a subject of intense investigation. Birds' night vision has been compared to ours, it is no better. Star maps seem to be used by some species, others are attuned to Earth's magnetic field and 'feel' their way like that.

All these questions, all these discoveries, are held in that one wood warbler in the April oak canopy at Horner, singing as if fit to burst. Simply looking at or listening to the bird might start anyone on a journey into understanding. From such understanding it is easy to see how love might grow. These days, it is unfashionable, perhaps even incorrect, to talk of love, but that cannot be legislated against. It happens. And I urge everyone who can, to get under those fresh green spring leaves to listen and look and have their hearts opened. ◆

(Pete Rae)

NIGHT ON EXMOOR

(Jen Rogers)

Rob Wilson-North **looks at historic perceptions of the dark.**

I remember sitting with Hope Bourne during an event in Frank Green's 'Hansel and Gretel'-like Music Room at Ashwick. Our conversation moved away from Frank Green's remarkable story and turned instead to the moors; we talked about prehistoric sites and the stories associated with them. Hope asked me if I had ever spent a night out on the moor alone. I said that I hadn't and she replied that, 'you need to, and then you will know the place and give credence to all the stories that you have read'.

Hope's passionate view of the moors can be balanced with the way that real, very real characters from the not-so-distant past experienced and lived with Exmoor at night. Ursula Halliday's wonderful history of her home, Glenthorne, includes an evocation of the brooding north facing coast of a moonlit Exmoor:

On both sides of the house,
the trees slide down the hills to
    reddish cliffs
and on clear nights,
the Nash Light shines on the walls
and the moon shines over the sea
through the branches of an old
    pine tree

That coastline, by accident of geography and history, ensured that Exmoor was both romantic but also a fruitful ground for smugglers. It was remote and rocky with few inhabitants; badly accessed by precarious roads and it lay on the northern side of a vast uninhabited, treeless waste: the old royal forest. Here the arm of the law stretching out from its county bases was at the very end of its extended fingertips. People could come and go, especially under the cover of darkness, generally without fear of hindrance. Such a nocturnal, clandestine activity is poorly documented and hard to research; nevertheless, in *Smuggling on the Exmoor Coast*, John Travis brings together the scant evidence for this busy activity. He relates that, in 1832: 'Part way through the night, the three Coastguard men saw a number of farmers with packhorses gathering on the beach. Lights flashed and a boat came to the shore laden with over 30 kegs of brandy.' And in 1853 a witness to the end of a long tradition reported that 'I sat by the deathbed of a very old smuggler who told me how he used to have a donkey with a triangle on its back so rigged up to show three lanthorns…watching on the Foreland for the three triangled lights of the schooner, which was coming in to land her cargo where Glenthorne now

stands and where there was a smugglers' cave…'. These smuggled goods, once ashore, could be dispersed over the landscape of the royal forest, which lay beyond the jurisdiction of local constabularies, and away into the darkness out across Devon and Somerset. So, by 1815, when the royal forest was enclosed by Act of Parliament, Exmoor had long been a centre for contraband distribution. When John Knight purchased the old royal forest in 1818 he upset the old order entirely.

Although John Knight had to work hard to impose his control on Exmoor, his son Frederic's problems were mainly financial. His long life was balanced between the Exmoor he loved, Worcestershire and London where, as an MP for 44 years, he lived in Dover Street and took his seat in the House of Commons. There he played a key role on the Poor Board. That long, full life made

"Sir Frederic Knight used to come over to Glenthorne and dine, then ride back across the moor to Simonsbath after 2 or 3 bottles of port."

him firm friends on Exmoor and in the reminiscences of Helen Cosway (one of the Halliday family of Glenthorne) written down in 1937, she recalls that 'Sir Frederic Knight used to come over to Glenthorne and dine, then ride back across the moor to Simonsbath after 2 or 3 bottles of port'. A rough calculation puts such a night time ride as 7 miles with an ascent of 1900 feet and a descent of 900 feet! Hardy moorland folk rose easily, it seems, to the challenges of the inky blackness of Exmoor…which, in Frederic Knight's case, was a far cry from Piccadilly!

In 1845 Frederic Knight leased Cornham Farm to William Hannan and his father. The Hannam family set off from Wiltshire and the account, below, of their horrendous journey onto Exmoor at night from Elworthy Cross at the eastern tip of the Brendon Hills, is taken from a recent performance of the Knight story scripted by Roger Watts and performed at Simonsbath House Hotel with Heather Hodgson:

> We had three wagons with three horses each and two carts with one horse each. We had two horses come to meet us at Handey Cross and two more of Mr Knight's at Raleigh's Cross [sic]. I had a covered carriage with my wife, servants and child with which we intended to get to Exmoor the same day, but could get no further than

Exford as the roads were in such a state after the severe frost… The horses could scarce get along so we got to Simonsbath the next morning. Here we left my family and returned to meet the wagons. I had expected to meet them at Cutcombe or Exford as they were going to travel all night. I rode to Raleigh's Cross where I found they had arrived some little time since having such difficulty to ascend Elworthy Hill. Having now fifteen horses and the stables but small, there was no room for more than 4 or 5 horses to lie down or feed. It was then 5 o'clock in a tremendous thick fog. I said to the men 'it is no use staying long here as there is no accommodation for the horses and night is coming on; we shall not see our way over the hills so our better way will be to get as soon as we can to Cutcombe.' Neither of the men knew the least part of the road and before we got half the distance it was so dark, we could not see a yard.

Glenthorn, 1860 (ENPA)

A feature of Exmoor in the past was its utter night-time darkness and I suspect that Hope Bourne was recalling such nights on the moor under the stars. Of course, in prehistory, the darkness would often have been complete. A feature of Exmoor's moorland landscape is the survival of extensive archaeological remains from the Neolithic and Bronze Ages. This physical evidence invites questions about the social history and beliefs of these communities. Elsewhere

> *"Perhaps Hope Bourne was right: that being alone on the moor at night helps bring the reality of those past lives nearer to us and the struggle of the everyday – or the everynight – to the fore."*

in the British Isles great communal monuments of the early Neolithic speak of an obsessive interest in the night sky and their alignment suggests a concerted effort to predict or acknowledge the year's cycle. They also speak of death and renewal, light and darkness. They are powerful cultural symbols.

On Exmoor, the great monuments of the early Neolithic are not found, which is of course interesting in itself. Instead, towards the later Neolithic and early Bronze Age (in the centuries either side of 2000BC) we encounter smaller structures: stone rows, stone circles and Exmoor's stone settings. Of these the stone circles on Porlock Allotment and Withypool Hill are, in common with small stone circles elsewhere, thought to be celestially aligned and in effect calendars of the seasons. The one at Porlock, lying within a landscape of prehistoric settlements was excavated in 2011. Further work will need to be done to establish any celestial orientation, but within the circle was found a lead votive offering deposited there maybe 1500 years after the circle was abandoned by a passing Roman and showing that such places had enduring meaning, but perhaps a departure from its original purpose. And so it is not unusual to find modern 'offerings' left there in the form of coins, shells and crystals. In common with the circles, Exmoor's stone rows and stone settings have never been studied in respect of their ritual function in relation to the night sky. The settings in particular would repay study.

Through the lives of people who lived in and used the moors in the past there is a raw, elemental quality about the place at night. In a modern world somehow now shielded from day-to-day survival, the anecdotes and stories of the past reconnect us with a world where life and death, hunger and plenty were very real. Perhaps Hope Bourne was right: that being alone on the moor at night helps bring the reality of those past lives nearer to us and the struggle of the everyday – or the everynight – to the fore. ◆

DR BRADSHAW'S BRIEF GUIDE TO BATS

Exmoor's dark skies, rural landscape and mosaic of habitats provide an ideal landscape for bats. Sixteen of the UK's eighteen native bat species have been recorded here.

Noctule (E Bradshaw)

Common pipistrelle (E Bradshaw)

Our largest species is the **noctule**, a tree-roosting bat that can weigh up to 40 g. Look for noctules around sunset flying high and fast above the tree canopy or over open ground. Their echolocation calls are low enough at 18 kHz to be heard by children. The related Leisler's bat, rarely reported on Exmoor, has calls that are easily confused with those of noctule and serotine, so may be under-recorded. Serotine bats roost almost entirely in buildings. They are widespread on Exmoor although breeding colonies are rarely found.

Common and soprano pipistrelles are the bats you are most likely to see. They often roost in crevices in houses, emerge early, have a distinctive fast, jerky flight and are fond of midges, eating up to 3,000 apiece a night. Nathusius's pipistrelle, a near-threatened migratory species, is far less common here.

Greater and **lesser horseshoe bats** are unusual in emitting sound through their nose (which has a horseshoe-shaped nose-leaf) rather than their mouth. They are agile fliers but can't move on the ground easily – hence they need large,

Lesser horseshoe hibernating (E Bradshaw)

enclosed spaces they can fly into, and grippy surfaces to hang upside down from. In summer they are often found in old buildings. In winter they hibernate in cellars, tunnels, mines and even sea caves, wrapping themselves in their wing membranes like strange fruit. Numbers declined by up to 90% over the last century, but are beginning to recover.

Barbastelle (H Lucking)

Brown long-eared (E Bradshaw)

The mothers change roost every few days, carrying their single pups with them. They are moth specialists, and with calls up to 100x quieter than other bats can catch moths that have evolved to 'hear' normal bat calls and take evasive action.

Natterer's maternity colony (E Bradshaw)

Brown long eared bats occur throughout Exmoor and breeding colonies often use buildings. The endangered grey long-eared bat is only found in Dunster and, more recently, Porlock Vale. The extraordinary ears, nearly as long as the body, are folded back at rest or tucked under the wings. Sensitive hearing and manoeuvrable flight allow these bats to hunt around vegetation, gleaning insects off surfaces.

Horner Wood is home to a breeding colony of the distinctive pug-nosed **barbastelle** bat. Considered vulnerable in the UK, this species prefers tree roosts.

Of the five *Myotis* species recorded on Exmoor, little is known about the distribution of Brandt's and Bechstein's bats. The other three species are widespread. Daubenton's bats fly low over ponds, rivers and lakes like small hovercraft, trawling for insects which they snatch off the surface with their large feet. **Natterer's** are woodland specialists but often roost in buildings, as do whiskered bats. ◆

TREES FOR THE WOODS

Georgina Macmillan, a young photographer studying photography at the University of the West of England, pays tribute to Exmoor's woods and trees.

Halscombe and Humbers Ball on Hawkridge Estate are virtually treeless, but from my bedroom window I can see this stand of Scots Pine and on the far ridge a plantation of conifers and broad leaves, known as Lords, a dark mark on the barren landscape. I have always loved the way trees stand out in solitude.

I took this photograph from where I live in Willingford ground using my digital Nikon D800 camera.

Hawkridge Estate (GM)

I took this photograph [opposite page) on a Leica R4 35-70mm, and the shallow depth of field means that the individual oak stands out from the other trees, a space surrounding it. It is is at Lankcombe near Badgworthy Water, where some of the trees have been ring dated to 500 years old. Trees are part of Exmoor's history and prehistory and native broadleaved woodlands covered most of Exmoor until they began to be cleared 7000 years ago, first for hunting and then agriculture and construction, hence why parts of moorland on Exmoor are called The Forest. This ancient natural woodland survived because its location made it inaccessible to machinery and transport. Badgworthy Land Company (founded 1926) now own Brendon Hill and the surrounding Forest moorland and let the veteran trees work out their own means of survival.

A collection of the dead, diseased and dying photographed in spring below Zeal Farm on Anstey Common. This picture shows how tough it is for trees on Exmoor. It is not just the weather they have to withstand, there is Acute oak decline and ash dieback, Fireblight killing rowan, Bark Beetle killing spruce, Phytophthora ramorum killing larch.

Dead, Diseased, Dying (GM)

Beech Hedge, Litton Farm (GM)

The remnant of a beech hedge at Litton Farm grounds, Little Hill. These grown out hedges are one of Exmoor's great sights. Originally six foot high, hedge banks were faced with stone and topped with turf. They were built by Frederic Knight to enclose the farm fields in the former Royal Forest his father John had bought in the 1820s. A full-time nursery man worked at Simonsbath to grow the beech whips that were planted in a double row along the top.

This was taken in early spring using an Olympus OM-1. I particularly like the way the film gives a sense of the murkiness of the moss.

A blasted Hawthorn on Blindwell Corner, Molland Moor that has adapted to cope with wind and rain, snow and ice, facing westerlies at 300 feet above sea level. Alone with moorland stretching for miles around, it is another defining Exmoor image. This was taken with a Nikon digital camera.

"The National Park plans to increase tree cover to about 17%."

Woodland covers about 14% of the National Park and a third is ancient woodland like this at Hawkridge Ridge. The National Park plans to increase tree cover to about 17%. It is putting in a new 12,000 tree wood on Bye Common above Winsford grown from locally sourced seed and 3,000 saplings went in at Timberscombe this May. There are plans for large scale planting along Exmoor's coastal strip and on steep ground, as part of the *England Woodland Creation Offer* to help build 'resilience against climate change.' If the government goal of 30 million new trees per year is to be met, we may not see the moor for the trees. *With thanks to Alice Nicholson for her additional research.* ◆

ONE SQUARE YARD OF BRENDON COMMON

Big things depend on little things. *Charles Foster*

(Anjelica Fraser)

For a year, on and off, I watched a square yard of Brendon Common, knowing that without the bacteria, protozoa, springtails and nematodes there would be no red deer, ravens or heather: none of the blazing glory of Exmoor. All big things depend on little things. If we could make soil as charismatic as lions, the conservation of the planet would be a good deal easier. Take away the micro-organisms that seethe in and on

"Take away the microorganisms that seethe in and on me and I'd be much lighter. I'd also be dead. Same for Brendon Common."

me and I'd be much lighter. I'd also be dead. Same for Brendon Common.

I marked the corners of the patch with stones. I took unsystematic soil samples and looked at them under a microscope. I rooted around with a trowel, cursing and apologising when I severed an earthworm. I knelt and peered through a lens, seeing glassy hairs and busy columns of mites where before I had seen only a blade of grass. I saw *that* blade of grass and *that* blade of grass where before I had seen only grass. I saw five species of grass where before I had seen only grass. Slowly I learned what I should have known from the human world: that there are only ever individuals, and that each individual is a densely woven web of relationships. Take away any of the defining relationships and the individual withers. Take away any significant number of those relationships and the individual dies.

The children thought I was mad and embarrassing. The little ones hadn't learned to doubt that there are only individual blades of grass, and didn't see the point of confirming it. The bigger ones had been disastrously convinced that categories – like 'grasses' and 'arthropods' are more important that individuals, and regarded my interest in specific hairs as childish and retarded. Yet even the older children gave names to the beetles we marked with spots of nail polish, and told stories about their travels.

In January a gale, born above the Sargasso when a spiralling wind from Cuba collided with a raft of dark cloud full of Orinoco water, flattened those grass blades and inoculated my square yard with a dose of tropical bacteria from the belly of a ballooning spider. Well, perhaps. You never know.

But what I do know is that Siberia responded, and made all the blades white and stiff for a bitter fortnight. Most of the little things made it underground, or

into cracks in logs and stones, before the land was locked. Some did not, but were held in the frost, their bodies bristling with ice crystals under my lens. It was warmer down below, and the deeper you went the more stable the temperature. Nine inches down, and Russia was irrelevant. There the nematodes (0.3 – 1mm long) hunted bacteria and protozoa and chewed fungal limbs and gobbets of plant bodies – mobilizing nutrients that had for a while been the borrowed property of particular things. In the spring (which seemed unthinkable to us, shivering by the gas fire), the molecules set free by the nematodes would be grafted into petals and pollen.

The cold forced the deer down from the hill. They huddled in the woods, living on their summer fat, slashing the ground with sharp feet in the hope of roots, and raiding turnip fields and gardens. One pile of

"One pile of dung, in the kindness of the wild gods, landed on my patch. It was poor stuff: thin and watery. But the heat of the deer's rectum summoned springtails and worms from far below."

dung, in the kindness of the wild gods, landed on my patch. It was poor stuff: thin and watery. But the heat of the deer's rectum summoned springtails and worms from far below. They raced for the surface and dived open-mouthed into the dung. Dung beetles, which can smell a good thing from a long way off, were there in hours. Three days later the dung was hollowed out from below, only a frozen crust remaining. Beneath was a labyrinth of tunnels – the nurseries of the fat dung-beetle larvae and the hunting grounds of the black beetles that grazed on them.

Then the unthinkable happened, as it always does. Right at the edge of the square – but overhanging the frontier, so that it seems fair to claim them – snowdrops pushed up and out. There must have been a moment when their tips were just visible, and then just slightly more visible, but it seemed to me that they exploded out of the dark in a moment – in the dead of night or the very early morning. For they were not there, I'm sure, when I went out in the evening, all muffled up, to sling a roadkill rabbit to the ravens and to smell the sour silage-breath of the deer. And then in the morning, when I went out to find that foxes had taken the rabbit, the flowers were defiantly there. What was the point? There were no pollinating insects, and wouldn't be for a while. The point can only be to convince me that the dark *always* fails.

These flowers had been forming for nine months. Tides of cells had been surging and curling down there amongst all the other tides of the soil. The flower tides had slowly curdled into a form, and the form had then been kneaded by genes and strange fields and the rasp of earthworm bristles until it was ready to blast between the clods and into the cold air of the Common. And that very first morning my daughter Rachel picked it and put it into a jam jar on the Rayburn and it was dead by sunset.

The deer dung changed the fortune of that square. A penumbra of life glowed around and under the dung – an oasis that fed and watered many from further afield. Carrion crows and starlings came to stab for beetle grubs, and a pied blackbird for earthworms. The crows, when the frost relented, probed half an inch down into soil that had formed at the time of the Armada.

Each predator thought it was just taking. But nothing ever *just* takes. Every visit left something behind, and everything that was left behind changed everything else for ever. The crows (my fancy insists) brought on their feet and their bills a luxuriant bacterial culture from the stomach of a poisoned fox which altered the digestion of a dynasty of earthworms. The blackbird must have found some old hawthorn berries by the stream, and two years later a tentative stalk nuzzled through a stockade of rye grass. I haven't been back since. Perhaps the hawthorn now has its own blackbird's nest.

> "*Each predator thought it was just taking. But nothing ever* just *takes. Every visit left something behind.*"

Those faecal berries brought bank voles, and one March night a tawny owl from the deep wood below the cottage dipped and gripped somewhere near the patch, and something wriggled on its way back to the owlets in an old beech.

The snowdrops formed a bridgehead, and the rest of the spring poured across it. The east wind crept back to Russia; the rain in the west wind dropped its cargo of caustic marine salt back into the sea rather than on the moor, and the land did not now shrink when it fell.

I had hoped for primroses in the square, but it was not to be, and I had to settle for three species of slug, seven species of beetle, three species of

earthworm, those five species of grass, many other plants, and an uncountable number of other types of things – things beyond my knowledge, eyesight, microscope-sight and imagination. But what a silly, artificial notion is the notion of a species. In a few million years, if the Earth survives, these species, so confidently described in the bird books, and given august Latin names, will have confounded our attempts to name and so control. They will have fragmented anarchically and unpredictably and magnificently, increasing still further the vertiginous variety of the world.

As it got warmer and less comfortable to lie at beetle-eye-level, the children took possession of the patch – or parts of it. Each child had a different jurisdiction – the result of strenuous and sometimes bloody negotiation. No one wanted the slugs, but Tom had the beetles, Jamie the other arthropods, Rachel (uncontentiously) all the plants, and Jonny the earthworms. 'Do you know', said Jonny, 'that the average age of earthworms is eight? That's older than me. And there are seven million earthworms for every human. This is *their* planet, not ours.' I was proud of that.

They inspected their stock with the diligence of a good shepherd. They mourned deaths and disappearances, and held detailed inquests. When the summer burned off Rachel's plants, the owners of the burrowers were smug. Jonny insisted that he could hear, with his ear to the ground, the scratch of the bristles as his earthworms pushed through the earth, each adult shoving aside boulders ten times its own weight. They learned about mycorrhizal fungi: how the tendrils in our

(Nigel Stone)

patch chatted chemically to those on the other side of the valley; how the valley was *one;* that it *knew.*

The children came to be glad when it rained, but shuddered with me at the approach of the cold. Their shuddering was different from mine. It had in it no fear of personal extinction or of the haemorrhage of colour or meaning that comes with depression. They knew, as I struggle to know, that colour only retreats and rests, and that meaning always *increases* as we go on living. The children shuddered because it made them warmer, which is the purpose for which shuddering is designed.

For me, when I looked out at the fog, and walked down to the East Lyn through a tangle of dripping branches, kicking the mould of leaves that had known willow warblers and now were being dragged underground in the fleshy mouths of ancient annelids, there was only despair.

Yet one morning in late December I lay down on a tarp for three aching hours, watching that one square yard of Brendon Common, feeling my heat seep down the tunnels made by Tom's beetles and Jonny's worms, seeing, even now, brave buds swelling on Rachel's plants. One of Jamie's viciously toxic centipedes crawled over my face in search of meat. Beneath and around there was no surrender or decay; just regrouping and rearrangement. There was comfort in this, as there was not in the walk through the big trees to the big cold river. There is comfort in the little things; in the particular. I need to start with those things. I need to start with a square yard and see where, if anywhere, I can go from there. ◆

(Nigel Stone)

MADE ON EXMOOR

Preserving this rare native pony has been a labour of local love by the moorland herd owners and the Exmoor Pony Society that celebrates its centenary this year. *Kate Green*

There is something irresistible about the Exmoor pony; the pleasing uniformity of a herd grazing windswept moorland speaks of romance, timelessness, antiquity. They certainly closely resemble the primitive equines that roamed the steppes in prehistoric times. But research by equine vet Peter Green in 2013 suggests that the ponies' standard appearance only really developed after the reclamation of the Exmoor Forest and was, in large part, due to the work of the Exmoor Pony Society.

The genesis of the Exmoor Pony Society (EPS) goes back to 1818, when the Crown sold the Royal Forest of Exmoor to the industrialist John Knight who 'civilised' the bleak open expanse with roads, fields and enclosures. The outgoing warden, Sir Thomas Acland, took the precaution of keeping 30 ponies to run on Winsford Hill – they became the famous Anchor herd, which is now owned by EPS vice-chairman David Wallace and his wife Emma. Other farmers followed suit and a handful of those herds still exist, such as the Milton family's Withypoole Herd 23.

By 1921, a group of farmers – from families like the Miltons, Westcotts and Darts that still own herds today – had become concerned that the true, sturdy Exmoor pony they rode staghunting, shepherding, or drove to market, would become unfashionable, subject to 'improvement' and the bloodlines diluted. They met in the Lion Inn, Dulverton, to form a stud-book, going to great lengths to select foundation stock and, by the 1930s, were travelling Exmoor Ponies by train to London for the big shows. Their work was nearly undone during the Second World War, when numbers on the moor dwindled to about 50 as ponies were shot, stolen for meat or wandered off. The recovery owes much to local breeder Mary Etherington, who rallied enthusiasm; safe moorland boundaries were restored through cattle grids and herds were re-established.

There are now some 500 ponies on Exmoor and around 3-4,000 in the world, but keeping the breed identity intact while at the same time maintaining enough genetic diversity is a huge challenge. In 2021 the Rare Breeds Survival Trust designated Exmoors as

"There are now some 500 ponies on Exmoor and around 3-4,000 in the world, but keeping the breed identity intact while at the same time maintaining enough genetic diversity is a huge challenge."

'priority' because of concerns about the genetics and, because the gene pool is finite, Exmoor's herds depend on injections from bloodlines maintained by breeders around the whole of the UK. They also require the exclusion of non-Exmoor ponies that can make their way into the breeding stock.

The Exmoor Pony Society (EPS) inspects and registers new foals, a process that can be controversial. Each autumn, herds are rounded up and the foals are DNA-tested by the Animal Health Trust and examined by EPS inspectors; it can be slow, bureaucratic and, if a foal is rejected, painful. Their criteria are the strictest of any breed society in the country, partly because there is no mechanism to include ponies that were left out of the original register and the identification process is extremely difficult. In 2018, concern about the impact this narrow pedigree register was having on the gene pool led some of the original 1921 herd owners, still breeding ponies on the moor, to establish the Moorland Exmoor Pony Breeders Group (MEPBG). This issues their own breed certificates. They are now working with the EPS, the National Park and the Rare Breeds Survival Trust to help secure the future of the breed.

The Gathering (Leanna Coles)

> *"Exmoors have always been versatile riding ponies, but it's the current rewilding zeitgeist that might prove their saviour."*

Exmoors have always been versatile riding ponies, but it's the current rewilding *zeitgeist* that might prove their saviour; the ponies 'natural' intelligence and useful physiognomy – the raised flesh around the (toad) eyes that protects from harsh weather, the double coat with greasy waterproof outer layer and the cast-iron digestions – has made them the perfect livestock for conservation grazing. There are Exmoor ponies at the rewilded Knepp Castle estate in West Sussex, at several National Trust sites and a family group has gone to Norfolk.

The EPS centenary celebrations have been largely online, but this year the breed show went ahead at Exford Show on August 11th celebrating these ponies – undeniably rare, locally distinctive and as totemic to the moor as its red deer. ◆

A longer version of this article appeared in Country Life magazine (26 May, Issue 2021).

MAKING SENSE OF ENVIRONMENT POLICY

To value Nature, the meaning of economic value needs to change. *Dr Keith Howe,* Deputy Chairman of the Exmoor Society

(Anjelica Tarnowska)

n June 2021, the Western Morning News published a column asking "Is the term 'biodiversity' being lost in translation?"[1]. It was reporting on the House of Lords committee stage discussion of the Environment Bill.[2] Questions had been raised about the choice of terms used in the Bill with the suggestion that 'biodiversity' should be replaced by 'nature'. The point was that people talk about nature, not biodiversity and that "Biodiversity is one of the worst examples of a pseudo intellectual word which most people do not understand and would never use in speech." In reply, it was explained that biodiversity has a more precise meaning. It encompasses everything about ecosystems "on which the natural environment depends and the diversity which gives it its life".

The Environment Bill will become an Act of Parliament; a legal document that must employ definitions whose meanings are as precise as possible. Meanings can and do change over time, sometimes because an existing meaning is misunderstood and becomes inadvertently redefined (such as 'iconic') or even inverted, such as in the schoolteacher's favourite example, "It's literally raining cats and dogs" – now that would be an environmental catastrophe! But more relevant here are new terms, coined to explain and interpret new perspectives on the world. That is the case with biodiversity and ecosystems.

BIODIVERSITY AND ECOSYSTEMS

'Biodiversity' is simply a contraction of biological diversity, just as 'ecosystems' is of ecological systems. Both are sources of the many goods and services necessary to sustain human life. When the term 'ecosystems' was first used in Exmoor Society debates it was greeted with nervous incomprehension by some; an understandable and healthy response as sometimes there is much less to a new or unusual concept than meets the eye. But here there is real significance, because by including respectively 'diversity' and 'systems' each contains the implication that complexity characterises the world. Why should this matter?

Over the past two centuries, thinking about the world has compartmentalised. Natural science (alternatively, natural philosophy) was partitioned into physics, chemistry, biology, and geology; social science, the focus of understanding how people behave and organise themselves in society, was subdivided into anthropology, economics, political science, psychology and sociology. Undoubtedly specialisation brought new and rich insights, but it also generated a kind of intellectual myopia. No one has expressed the consequences of this disciplinary fragmentation better than Thor Heyerdahl:

> In order to penetrate ever further into their subjects, the host of specialists narrow their field and dig down deeper and deeper till they can't see each other from hole to hole. But the treasures their toil brings to light they place on the ground above. A different kind of specialist should be sitting there, the only one still missing. He would not go down any hole but would stay on top and piece all the different facts together.[3]

In universities today the different facts are being pieced together. Practitioners of natural and social science work with each other, the humanities too, pooling expertise and unique insights to address issues of common interest; evidence abounds of reorientation towards collaborative effort. If we are to address environmental problems with the urgency they so desperately need, everyone must understand why it is essential to take the wide view.

ENVIRONMENT POLICY TODAY

A glance at the Environment Bill 2021 confirms the sheer breadth of issues that occupy decision makers. It covers waste and resource efficiency, air and water quality, drainage, biodiversity, nature

"... the Environment Bill 2021 confirms the sheer breadth of issues that occupy decision makers. It covers waste and resource efficiency, air and water quality, drainage, biodiversity, nature recovery, conservation, habitats, and trees."

recovery, conservation, habitats, and trees. The prologue to the Bill refers to improving the natural environment *for connected purposes* (emphasis added). Expressed another way, the different elements, or subsystems are all part of an overarching system of complex ecosystem relationships. Each element needs to be understood in isolation, as it stands alone, but also in terms of its relationships and higher purpose. The total environment can be properly understood only by investigating its behaviour as more than the sum of its individual parts.

The government's 25 Year Environment Plan[4] set out the broad strategy objectives. Subsequently, the Agriculture Act 2020[5], the Landscapes Review[6], the Dasgupta Review[7], statements from the National Capital Committee[8] and contributions to environment debates from numerous independent sources have all helped to refine ideas and understanding. At the same time, they leave a sense of being overwhelmed by the deluge of ideas, recommendations and policies. Most challenging of all is how to decide what to do for maximum benefit, both for the environment and, by implication, for ourselves. That task needs careful consideration of what it is that people value most about the environment, and how much. Biodiversity, key signifier of environmental health, occupies prime position in addressing that question.

THE DASGUPTA REVIEW

An independent review on the economics of biodiversity was led by Professor Sir Partha Dasgupta, Emeritus Professor of Economics at Cambridge University. Its purposes were to a) assess the economic benefits of biodiversity, b) assess the economic costs and risks of biodiversity loss and c) identify a range of actions that can simultaneously enhance biodiversity and deliver economic prosperity. To paraphrase Dasgupta's main messages, biodiversity enables Nature (capitalisation is significant) to be productive, resilient, and adaptable. Nature, the term he uses interchangeably with natural capital, natural resources, the natural environment, the biosphere, and the natural world, is fundamental. Diversity reduces risk and uncertainty, increases resilience to shocks and so the risks to availability of the services Nature provides. By reducing biodiversity, Nature and humanity both suffer. We and our economies are embedded in Nature, not external to it, something we seem to forget until Nature reminds us, often with dramatic force.

NATURE'S WORTH

A problem is that Nature's worth to society – the *true* value of the various goods and services (ecosystem services) it provides – is not reflected in market prices. Values based on market prices have been called 'subjective values' because people reveal their preferences by decisions they make on which goods and services they choose to spend their money. In the modern world, 'value' has become synonymous with monetary valuation and, therefore, if something has no money value it may be treated as valueless.

But Nature is different, it has 'intrinsic value' because everything else depends on it. This includes the public goods, such as those listed in the Environment Bill, which have received so much attention in recent years. A characteristic of public goods is that it is not possible to translate their value into the directly observable money equivalents that normal market prices provide. The true values of their costs and benefits are therefore invisible, apparently (and erroneously) zero. And if a resource is costless, it means it must be so abundant that it can be used without limit. Consequently, Nature – the mother of all resources – is overexploited and damaged.

To put it another way, society fails to

" … society fails to pay the true costs of acquiring the benefits from Nature because we are deluded into believing they come free."

pay the true costs of acquiring the benefits from Nature because we are deluded into believing they come free or, at best, are bought for a monetary outlay that does not account for all relevant costs. The imperfect ability of money prices to capture true values means that

market activity leads to socially undesirable outcomes. For instance, higher yields obtained by a farmer adding nitrogen fertiliser to a crop (a benefit of evident value to him) typically fail to account for the costs of excess nitrate run-off into nearby water courses (eutrophication, polluted water extracted for drinking undermining human health). Only the monetary cost of the fertiliser is accounted for, not the additional costs (negative value) of its unwanted side-effects.

Nature is so fundamental to human existence that without nurturing it we cannot satisfactorily provide for the life-sustaining needs and wants of either present or future generations. Further, caring for Nature may also be a moral obligation, for many people perhaps underpinned by reverence for what is considered God-given. Where Nature is valued beyond conventional monetary measure, Dasgupta argues, it should be protected by decree. It is typically less costly to conserve Nature than to restore it. But to achieve that aim means we need major transformative change in decision-making institutions underpinned by ambition, coordination and political will:

The transformative change needed in choosing the sustainable path requires the sustained commitment of actors at all levels. It also involves hard choices. Standard economic models view our choices as self-centred. There is growing evidence, however, that our preferences are affected by the choices of others – they are 'socially embedded'.

"The transformative change needed in choosing the sustainable path requires the sustained commitment of actors at all levels. It also involves hard choices (Dasgupta)."

Simonsbath, Chaos of Light
(Jo Minoprio, Arborealists)

EXMOOR SOCIETY'S ROLE

The context of Dasgupta's Review is global but, consistent with the view that understanding the entire system needs close attention to its parts, relevant to Exmoor is reference to the need to expand and improve the management of protected areas. Multi-functional landscapes and seascapes that provide ecosystem goods and services, and protect and enhance biodiversity, are important. Large-scale and widespread investment in Nature-based solutions would help address biodiversity loss and significantly contribute to climate change mitigation and adaptation. Wider economic benefits include job creation.

At the time of writing, news media are reporting the frightening impact of the North American heat dome and floods in Germany, Belgium, the Netherlands, Switzerland, and China. If there now, why not here in the future? Since its inception, the Exmoor Society has supported like-minded organisations, notably the National Park Authority, in the task of ensuring that the Statutory Purposes for our national parks are observed. These embrace conservation, enhancing natural capital, preserving cultural heritage, and enabling inhabitants and visitors to benefit from an exceptionally tranquil and beautiful environment. In summary, it seeks to enhance Exmoor's provision of highly valued biodiversity and ecosystems. Now, with overwhelming evidence of climate change brought about by human failure to value Nature as we should, a new dimension is added: attention to the science of climate change and of how it may affect Exmoor's landscape. On that foundation, the Exmoor Society will continue to make its own contribution aimed at influencing decisions taken for Nature's betterment in the place we hold so dear. ◆

1 Western Morning News, June 23, 2021, page 13
2 https://bills.parliament.uk/bills/2593
3 Thor Heyerdahl, 1958. Aku-Aku. The Secret of Easter Island. George Allen & Unwin Ltd., pages 357-8.
4 https://www.gov.uk/government/publications/25-year-environment-plan & /25-year-environment-plan-progress-reports
5 https://www.legislation.gov.uk/ukpga/2020/21/contents/enacted/data.htm
6 https://www.gov.uk/government/publications/designated-landscapes-national-parks-and-aonbs-2018-review
7 https://www.gov.uk/government/publications/final-report-the-economics-of-biodiversity-the-dasgupta-review
8 https://www.gov.uk/government/groups/natural-capital-committee

TO SHEAR WELL

Dr John Wibberley tells an Exmoor yarn of services to sheep

Raised on the high standards of Victorian craftsmanship, my grandfather would constantly say, '*If a job's worth doing, it's worth doing well*', and shearing sheep is worth doing well. Part of the rhythm of farm life, it is done for the sheep's welfare to prevent fly strike and keep them cooler in summer and, at least historically, for the value of the wool clip. Sheep, their meat and their wool, have long played a central role shaping the British economy and landscape and in few places more so than Exmoor.

Other than the notable exceptions of the auto-shedding *Exlana* (a recently created composite breed) and the small flocks of 'hand plucked' Soays on the Western Isles, British sheep get shorn. In late May to early June, shearers do the rounds, rolling countless sheep onto their rumps and clipping them close before bagging up the wool and moving on. The British record, set in 2019 by Stuart Connor, is for 785 lambs in 9 hours, just 82-short of the world record. The fleeces used to be valued: the Woolmen, one of the oldest Guilds in the City of London, was set up in 1180 to ensure high standards in the production and marketing of wool and is still operating. In Plantagenet times (1154-1485) the price of wool was so high that along with wheat it was a barometer of English farming's prosperity. In the limestone areas of the South Downs and Cotswolds many historic churches and manor houses were built on the proceeds of wool, and Dunster's Yarn Market and well-built houses are a measure of the economic importance it had for Exmoor. However, following the introduction of nylon and other synthetic fibres in the late 1930s, the price of wool declined sharply. There are times that the price barely covers the cost of the clip although it is still valued as a natural fibre for clothes and building insulation – and sheep still need shearing…

Roll forward a century from my grandfather's youth, and an Exmoor farmer's son, Richard Webber, starting out on his working life in Cutcombe learned to shear on the family flock of about 120 sheep. Following a well-trodden Exmoor path, in 1978 he went to New Zealand – a place where there is plenty of work for a sheep farmer. In the 1970s and early 1980s sheep outnumbered people 20:1 in New Zealand. Although deregulation and the removal of state support for agriculture in 1985-6 led to a sheep population crash, even now humans are massively outnumbered: there are 30 million sheep and 4.4M people, a ratio of 6 to 1. Not surprising then that New Zealand was where Richard Webber went looking for work, nor that it was the place the great revolution in sheep shearing occurred.

Farmer Godfrey Bowen (1922-94) was the unexpected pioneer. A Christian, he had prayed for answers to the two great blights of shearing – sheep being cut and bruised and the high level of waste in the wool clipped – and his concern for sheep welfare and good uniform wool quality led him to develop his now world-

Godfrey Bowen

Richard Webber and family

famous Bowen Method. After years of shearing, observation and testing, Bowen realised that by seating the sheep comfortably and turning it smoothly, the non-shearing hand is free to stretch out the skin which makes it far less liable to be pinched and cut. In 1953, Bowen set a world shearing record – 456 full wool ewes in 9 hours at Manawatu, North Island and became a national hero. He was appointed the New Zealand Wool Board's chief training instructor, began running university shearing courses, gave demonstrations at agricultural shows and promoted shearing as a spectator sport. In the years that followed his world record the Bowen Method went global. He travelled from South Africa to Japan, shearing as he went. In 1960 he was made an MBE and in 1963, at the height of the Cold War, Russian President Nikita Khruschev, a shepherd's son himself, honoured Bowen with a Star of Lenin and as a Hero of Labour for teaching his method to Russian shepherds.

This was the heady atmosphere of NZ sheep and shearing that Richard Webber

breathed when he arrived from Exmoor. He had learned left-handed and right-handed shearing at home where shearers used catchers, but aged 15 he had witnessed Godfrey Bowen catch his own sheep and shear them blindfold in a much discussed demonstration at Wheddon Cross and that was what he wanted to do too. After two seasons in New Zealand, he had won bronze, silver and then gold awards at the NZ Schools of Shearing. Richard also spent seven seasons working in Norway where, shearing in an abattoir, he noticed that their closed loop ear tags, unlike many of those on Exmoor, didn't get tangled in wire and fall off. Inspired by all he had learned in NZ and Norway, Richard returned home to Exmoor determined to put it into practice.

His first enterprise was to acquire a trailer and, towing it around Exmoor with a contract gang of 25 shearers, offer shearing, dipping and other sheep-care services. This gave him a wide experience of sheep husbandry on Exmoor and the improvements that would make it more competitive. His great insight was how important it was to be able to reliably identify your sheep and how this would mean that they were traceable both in the field and food chain – with the bonus that the information could be used for improved breeding management and disease monitoring. While wise managers recognise that some of the most important aspects of life are immeasurable, Richard Webber intuitively realised that farmers need to follow the business maxim: *measure it to manage it.*

He set about solving the ear tag problem and in 1990 founded *Shearwell* Data. His

Exmoor Horn (© Jonathan Delafield Cook, courtesy Purdy Hicks Gallery)

timing was perfect; EU obligations to identify each sheep for administrative and compliance purposes and the outbreak of Foot-And-Mouth Disease in the UK in 2001 meant that the market for tags took off. The 2000s also marked the start of the digital revolution in agriculture as it

became apparent that technology could be used to record both increasingly large flock numbers and management information about the individual sheep. With the mission 'to improve data collection, traceability and profitability for farmers, with products that are easy to use' *Shearwell* pioneered electronic identification (EID) of livestock and then went on to develop associated equipment such as Digital Measuring Sticks, Automatic Drafting Crates, *Shearwell* EID Weigh Crates, and the *Te Pari Racewell* Sheep handling system that allows livestock farmers to record and shed their sheep swiftly. *Shearwell* tags and EID equipment are now found not just on Exmoor and in the UK but across the world in Australia, Canada, Ireland, New Zealand, Saudi Arabia and the USA. Just as the Bowen Method transformed sheep husbandry fifty years ago, today it is *Shearwell* data.

Author's Note:

Shearwell, now managed by the next generation of Webbers, employs 100 people in the National Park, and from its office and factory outside Wheddon Cross contributes some £3.5M annually to Exmoor's economy and offers easy access to its world leading technology to Exmoor's farmers. Building a business like this in the protected landscape of a National Park has not been without challenges. However, with a cooperative attitude from both the planners and the business, a way forward has been found that has allowed a light industrial business to flourish. Without a thriving rural economy and community, National Park conservation and access mandates cannot be maintained. ◆

EXMOOR PILGRIMS

Camper vans, caravans, motor homes: the freedom of the road is irresistible to a new kind of traveller – and they are slowly wending your way… *George Macpherson*

THE CONVERTS

Last year they came in their hundreds, in shiny white, carrying all that they needed on their racks. They stopped on the roadsides and by rivers and, taking down their bicycles, canoes and paddle boards journeyed on to commune with Mother Nature. They are Exmoor's latest visitors, its new pilgrims. No longer footsore, carrying staffs and bundles or even dressed in tweed and swept around in Range Rovers, but rather comfortable in shorts and hoodies, in gleaming mobile bubbles heading west down the M5 on socially distanced journeys.

£10,000 to £100,000 may seem excessive: the kind of money that should go towards a holiday chalet, or the deposit for a cottage. Instead, each year 14,000 people spend the family savings or the newly increased mortgage on motor homes and the freedom of the road. There are around 225,000 motor homes in the UK labouring slowly up hills, swerving to avoid low hanging branches, sailing past every layby and accelerating when the road straightens out. Kent for Easter, Norfolk for Whitsun and why not Exmoor for the summer?

The happy campers, the caravan of pilgrims, trundle around the country carrying all they need for day-to-day living – hot water, air conditioning, shower, loo, kitchen with fridge cooker and hob, microwave, television, Wi-Fi, comfortable beds, dining room, armchairs. For better weather, awnings unfold, deck chairs and the bikes are unloaded from the back of the nine-metre-long monsters. Some even tow a small car so that they can travel around and explore anywhere from Treborough to Tippacott without unsettling their movable home.

"For better weather, awnings unfold, deck chairs and the bikes are unloaded from the back of the nine-metre-long monsters."

In times of plague it is the perfect escape. After months of lock down in towns and cities, working at home, schooling at home, exercising at home staring at the same four walls; not being able to stretch eyes, limbs and lungs; and unable to go abroad, the mobile home is liberty. A holiday without having to breathe the air of strangers. At the start of 2020 one of the largest local dealers, Chelston Motor Homes of Wells, thought they were facing catastrophe. By May business was blazing, motor homes burning rubber as they accelerated out of the door. When they finally stopped, when their new owners reached the moor, the clean air, rich woods and pastures, they walked, rode and often followed John Ridd's path in his wooing of *Lorna Doone*, through Dulverton, Bridgetown and Dunkery Beacon and on in search of the secret Doone Valley. Some spent time chilling by the Barle or Exe while the young ones splashed in the pure water. Then it was easy – back into the home that came with them, right there with its full fridge, grocery cupboard and comfortable beds.

ARE THE PILGRIMS READY FOR EXMOOR?

The pleasure is in the planning. Join the RAC, AA, the Caravan and Motor Home Club, or the oldest one, the Caravan Club and, for about £50 a year, members get maps and magazines full of forthcoming events and reviews of the latest models and refinements. They also get the invaluable book of contacts for the hundreds of sites to choose from. On Exmoor there are around thirty, half of which are open all year round and with the book on your knees you can dream – you can choose the sea in Combe Martin, the sessile oak woods of north Exmoor, or to cling to the side of Winsford Hill. Then there are those who don't read the manuals or feel that camp sites are for them, who think that the freedom of the road is the freedom to pull up anywhere and then move on, sometimes leaving quite a lot behind them so that everyone else knows where they have been.

IS EXMOOR READY FOR THEM?

But do Exmoor residents and businesses make the most of these newcomers? Many mobile home and camp sites close down during the winter but even this doesn't completely stem the flow of these ungainly white monsters,

stop them from blocking the roads, clearing the shelves in the village store on a Friday night and last winter, 'bringing the virus'. With the release that vaccines bring there is likely to be a second and much larger wave that could be a useful source of income for Exmoor farmers, landowners and even home owners with barns or secure parking places. The post-Covid relaxation of the planning regulations means that pitches can be offered for 56 days a year without the need for planning permission and £16-20 can be charged per vehicle per week in addition to a fee per person. There are possible other earners once the farm family has got to know their 'tenants' – such as offering a single site with plug in and disposal facilities.

THE JOURNEY

There are two kinds of pilgrim, the solitary and the social. There are the travellers who join in the site community, take part in Club activities, meet for drinks and enjoy regular meetings with

> *"Men and women working as lawyers and doctors park up next to street sweepers – and arrange to meet them again next year."*

like-minded people. I have been amazed at the atmosphere when I arrive at sites, friendly and without snobbery or class barriers. Men and women working as lawyers and doctors park up next to street sweepers – and arrange to meet them again, 'next year if you're coming this way,' bonding over knowledge of 'how to

stop the wagon from getting too hot at two in the morning' or 'how to get rid of that awful smell in the shower cubicle'. Pets generally join in too and get to know each other without disgracing their owners although uncontrollable dogs or ferrets have been known to cause problems. These people have their favourite sites and book up well in advance, often at the same time each year, so that the little community or caravan (collective noun for pilgrims) can meet again. And they will have plenty to discuss since their last enjoyable break in the country and plenty to show each other too; their latest upgrade that has cost them another £8,000, "But do just look! It is 'self-levelling'".

Lone travellers are the other group. They are the hermits who seek out the solitude of an empty site and don't mind the cold and rain of out of season breaks. While other owners have mothballed their vehicles, jacked them up and taken the batteries home until Easter, they scour the Caravan Club listings for obscure sites that are open all year. On dark February weekends they set off for wind swept fields, overjoyed to find them empty and delighted to lie at night, in a completely new place, protected and warm in their pure white vans while the gale gently rocks them to sleep. ◆

ZOOMOLOGY

I zoom, thou zoomest, she zooms, he zooms –
As children we zoomed in the playground
When mimicking cars of a speedy design
We adopted such noises befitting them fine.
There's an etiquette to it – to zooming I mean,
For a start, it's the background domestic'lly seen,
Some – the crafty ones – backdrop a wondrous fake scene
Of faraway mountains or beaches serene.
Then there's rules for the hobby of reading book titles
On shelves of the zoomers while they do recitals.
Of course, when you're zooming, no food can be shared
But some zoomers chew freely, their fellows not spared;
When all's said and done, zooming has been a boon,
But let's hope we'll meet face-to-face sensibly soon!

EJW

Exmoor's farmsteads

The collection of traditional farm buildings that accompany each farmhouse are a distinctive feature of our landscape. Familiar, vernacular, sometimes planned, sometimes gently haphazard, they shape our sense of the farmed landscape. Although most of Exmoor's farms are ancient, most of these familiar groups of buildings have only emerged in the last 200 years or so, to work in harmony with the individual landholding that they served. As such they formed part of a highly efficient organism in which farm processes flowed through the moors and woodlands to the farmland and farmstead and back again in a virtuous cycle. But now many of these buildings have fallen into disuse or are being repurposed and the farming systems that they formed a part of are rapidly transforming in the face of 21st century pressures. In response to this, the Exmoor National Park Authority and the Exmoor Society are exploring how the farming systems that have given rise to so much that is distinctive, loved and protected in the Exmoor landscape, evolved and functioned. Farmers' memories, diaries, photographs, hay meadows, field boundaries and the humble stone buildings of an Exmoor farmstead all have their part in the story to tell. And of these, perhaps the humblest is the linhay. ◆

Rob Wilson-North

Coombe Farm (ENPA)

Stetfold Rocks Farm, Exford (ENPA)

A MATTER OF PRIDE

Linhays are modest and often unnoticed but they are part of the West Country's landscape character. *Annabel Barber*

Ask a person to describe the Exmoor landscape, and they will typically reach for words like "grandeur" or "majestic". It is understandable: this may be a managed wilderness, but nature makes itself felt here. Mankind's determination to tame his environment has led to easy wins in some parts of the world; not so on Exmoor. Human constructions, on the whole, are not grand and soaring like the cliffs, nor expansive and sweeping like the moor. They are huddling and hunkered: stone settings made of mini- rather than megaliths; tiny churches tucked away from major sight-lines; packhorse bridges tailored to fit the smallest cob and cart. Even those mighty engineers the Romans only managed a couple of "fortlets".

"*'Tis not for pride this little work I did, but it was for necessity and need.*" So reads a plaque on an old farmhouse near Wimbleball. Nature is grand and majestic here, but our makeshift human works are modest. Yet in an age when there are anxious calls for us to curtail our expansion, to rewild, to focus on natural capital, tone down our pride and content ourselves with bare necessities, the inhabitants of Exmoor are better placed than many to respond.

In 1823, on one of his *Rural Rides*, William Cobbett observed the following, near Margate:

I got to a little hamlet, where I breakfasted; but could get no corn for my horse, and no bacon for myself! All was corn around me. Barns, I should think, two hundred feet long; ricks of enormous size and most numerous; crops of wheat, five quarters to an acre, on the average; and a public-house without either bacon or corn! The labourers' houses all…beggarly in the extreme. The people dirty, poor-looking; ragged. Invariably have I observed, that the richer the soil, and the more destitute of woods; that is to say, the more purely a corn country, the more miserable the labourers. The cause is this, the great, the big bullfrog grasps all…every inch of land is appropriated by the rich. No hedges, no ditches, no commons, no grassy lanes: a country divided into great farms…and the wretched labourer has not a stick of wood, and has no place for a pig or cow to graze, or even to lie down upon. The rabbit countries are the countries for labouring men. There the ground is not so valuable. There it is not so easily appropriated by the few.

Size matters, and historically it has often been an advantage to be too small to bother with. An Exmoor hill farm, suited to livestock, not grain, has a difficult topography that puts a brake on its dimensions and deters greedy eyes. It is not easy to collectivise the uplands: this is a part of the world where individual resilience, independence and self-

Leigh Farm Linhay (Miranda Johnston)

sufficiency are the norm. Thus a typical Exmoor farmhouse is small and low-slung, its outbuildings diminutive. Up on the moor, the sheepfolds are compact: the fine circular one at Three Combes Foot, with the beech trees on top of the banks now grown into a tall arboreal cupola, measures less than twenty yards across. Near Gupworthy is the deserted medieval hamlet of Smarmoor, shrunk now to a few humps in the field and an abandoned, roofless barn. Close by, there is another ruin: gaunt stone walls and the collapsed debris of a slate roof. It is marked on the Ordnance Survey map as "Young's Linhay".

A linhay (pronounced linny), is a small and always, open-fronted agricultural shed or livestock shelter, is unique to the English west country. As the *hórreo* is to Galicia in north-west Spain or the brick-grilled *pareti grigliate* to the haylofts

of northern Italy, so the linhay is to Somerset, Dorset, Devon and Cornwall. All three constructions aim to fulfil the same need and solve the same problems: provide shelter and storage, keeping out the damp while allowing air to circulate. The linhay has a venerable history. It even has its place in literature:

Tim descended the path to the back of the house…and reaching the wall he stopped. Owing to the slope of the ground, the roof-eaves of the linhay were here within touch, and he thrust his arm up under them, feeling about in the space on the top of the wall-plate.

'Ah, I thought my memory didn't deceive me!' he lipped silently.

With some exertion he drew down a cobwebbed object curiously framed in iron, which clanked as he moved it. It was about three feet in length and half

Red Cross Linhay

as wide. Tim contemplated it as well as he could in the dying light of day, and raked off the cobwebs with his hand.

'That will spoil his pretty shins for'n, I reckon!' he said.

It was a man-trap.

The passage comes from Thomas Hardy's *The Woodlanders* (1887). Before he turned to writing, Hardy was an architect, and this training, together with his Dorset upbringing, meant that the terms "linhay" and "wall-plate" were self-explanatory to him. Not, perhaps, to all his readers. A wall-plate is a horizontal beam that distributes the load of the (linhay) roof. The space beneath it can form a useful hidey-hole for things like man-traps. If more general storage space is needed, a separate upper level can be constructed in a linhay, with planks and beams. This gives the linhay its typical features.

Like all traditional Exmoor farm buildings, made for a landscape that cannot support vast agri-concerns, linhays are modest in size. Usually they are rectangular, but L-shaped examples can be found and at Braunton, near Barnstaple, there is a round one. For storage, many linhays have an upper level made of wood, sometimes stretching the full depth of the building but often taking the form of a gallery or shelf at the back. There is a spectacular horseshoe-shaped linhay near Brompton Regis, with its upper storey still intact, and filled—when I last saw it—with a jumble of *bric à brac* and old lumber, including an ancient upright piano. One could easily

" … when you start to look for linhays, you realise they are everywhere."

imagine a man-trap there.

Linhays were often roofed with thatch. More commonly today, this has been replaced with slate or corrugated iron. There are even some, make-do-and-mend style, covered with asphalt roll. The roofs are supported either on wooden posts or by pillars of stone which in themselves are marvels of construction. They take the form of stout cylindrical columns, as fat as elephants' legs, made of loose rubble piled carefully in layers and secured with mortar. Typically, it seems that the whole column was then rendered, though the render is in many cases now crumbling away. How these columns stand firm; how they have sufficient integrity to support the weight, is miraculous. The stones themselves are plentiful. Anyone who has tried to dig a flower bed or a vegetable garden will know full well that you cannot put spade to soil here without encountering rocks. Some of them are small and round as a Jersey Royal, some of them are flat, some of them are as big as tombstones. All make excellent locally-sourced, low-mileage linhay-building material.

And when you start to look for linhays, you realise they are everywhere. Many old farms have more than one, sometimes in the main yard, sometimes out in the fields—in which case a paved or cobbled court was often created in front of them, to prevent poaching of the ground. John Knight built some on the Exmoor Forest, as did the Aclands at Holnicote. There is a small one beside the lane to Hartford, still to this day used for sheltering sheep. At another small farm in the same area, the sheds that surround the yard, built only a few years ago by a farmer who was a skilled stonemason, were built by him instinctively in the traditional lean-to linhay shape.

But economies of scale in one respect lead to size inflation in another. As the number of hands on a farm shrinks and the size of the machinery grows, so the buildings in the yard get larger – completely dwarfing the dwelling house in many cases. First there was the Dutch barn; now there is the pole barn:

"The tall, spacious hangars that the modern farmer needs are on a different scale from the tiny linhays."

practical, easy to construct and universal. The tall, spacious hangars that the modern farmer needs are on a different scale from the tiny linhay, impractical now except for the needs of smallholders. Flocks are too numerous; modern hay bales too galumphing. You could perhaps use a linhay to garage a small Goldoni tractor, such as they use in Italy to fit neatly between the rows of a vineyard. A standard John Deere, though? Impossible. In any case, the spates of rural theft mean that most farmers like to lock their valuables up. The open-fronted linhay is useless.

Which brings us on to how linhays have been adapted. Exmoor winters might be mild compared to the north and east of the country, but the trees do not leaf in many parts of the area until May. So it is not unusual to see a linhay where the spaces between the pillars have been filled in with a wooden screen or curtain wall, to create at least one section that is fully enclosed. Many surviving linhays are being altered to fit other modern uses too, converted into guest houses, studio workshops, home offices, or simply repurposed as garages and lumber sheds.

To survive, then, the linhay needs to

Riphay Linhay (Miranda Johnston)

evolve. We cannot expect a modern shepherd to go on using his linhay, forgoing convenient open-plan barns, any more than we can expect a dairy farmer to carry on maintaining a picturesque milkchurn table. Milkchurn tables have all gone, and many linhays are disappearing too.

Historic maps mark "court and linhay" or "linhay and barton" in numerous places where all trace of a building has now vanished. Plenty of others are ramshackle or falling down. At Porlock, where the salt marsh has reclaimed the fields, the fine old L-shaped linhay, with an expansive intact loft storey, stands derelict.

An awareness of what these buildings are, of their uniqueness and their traditional place in this environment, can go a long way to helping us to treasure

them and thus safeguard the future of those that still stand. Everyone knows what a chalet is, or an oast house. Why not a linhay? A recent sale advertisement for an Exmoor fish farm describes its two main buildings as an "eighteenth-century barn" and a "bungalow".

Look at the accompanying photo gallery, though, and you realise that both buildings are in fact converted linhays, with beautiful rubble-stone and mortar columns. Surely this is something that everyone needs to know? Instead of beguiling potential buyers with the promise of a "bungalow" (so faceless and generic!), why not tempt them with a "converted linhay", something imbued with a proper sense of place? This is not just a case of necessity and need. It is a matter of pride. ◆

WELCOME TO EXMOOR

Is Exmoor too beautiful for its own good.
Kate O'Sullivan

Sherdon Water (Clover Godsal)

In the mist of pre-Covid life, when holidays involved airports and the baking sun, the Glover Landscapes Review was published. Its remit: to find out where designated landscapes were succeeding, where failing and recommend ways that they could do better.

National Parks have two equal purposes: to conserve and enhance the natural beauty, wildlife and cultural heritage of the National Parks and to promote opportunities for the public understanding and enjoyment of the special qualities of the Parks. Glover's two main recommendations are responses to these. He called for a new commitment to recover and enhance nature, one that puts natural beauty at is core, and he called for these landscapes to fulfil their original post war mission to connect all people with our national landscapes for their 'enjoyment, spiritual refreshment …health and wellbeing."[1]

It is an exciting and optimistic vision in which the terrifying decline of species, climate warming and the destruction of natural beauty and landscapes are, if not reversed, at least halted in these precious places. In tandem with this the report

> *"The sun shone and often first-time visitors… came and sat by rivers and picnicked, waded, splashed and gazed at the birds, rode their bikes and horses, paddled and kayaked."*

asks that the parks and AONBs reach out to and welcome 'particular and significant communities that make up modern Britain'. Children will be inspired to respect and save nature; a ranger service will ensure that new audiences are welcome and the open spaces will be a kind of giant adventure playground that can be used to improve physical and mental health at a low cost.

Exmoor usually has 2 million visitors per year – although last year based on their car parks, the Exmoor National Park Authority (ENPA) think there was an increase of about 30%. Others, who counted the cars that parked on verges,

estimate something more like 70%. The sun shone and often first-time visitors, from groups more widely representative of society, came and sat by rivers and picnicked, waded, splashed and gazed at the birds, rode their bikes and horses, paddled and kayaked. It was a joyful escape from the imprisonment of Covid and there was a sense that Exmoor was fulfilling its role as a park for everyone. But this fantastic success – and one that in many ways makes Glover's call for wider access redundant – also exposed the fundamental conflict between the two purposes of the parks and likewise his two calls for reform.

Over the last year the Exmoor Society has carried out their own landscapes review on Exmoor – mainly at honey pots – trying to understand the impact visitors have and ways that the contradiction within the Glover Review, between the two purposes of National Parks, can be reconciled. The Exmoor Society looked at Horner Wood, Porlock Marsh, Woody Bay and Landacre Bridge. These areas are in National Nature Reserves (NNR), Sites of Special Scientific Interest (SSSI) and Special Areas of Conservation (SAC) – this means that they include some of the rarest and most important habitats in the country and have been designated with protection 'to make sure that nature and wildlife aren't harmed or destroyed'[2]. The same problems were identified at all of them – litter, excrement, dogs putting up nesting birds and dogs in rivers, noise, light, fires, overnight camping, off road vehicles and bikes turfing up and eroding the ground. Adventure activities involving kit seemed particularly problematic – jet skis off Woody Bay scaring cliff birds, bike events down Dunkery scaring everyone, off-roaders roaring round Stoke Pero, kayakers on Porlock Marsh.

Site:

Horner Wood

Horner wood is an exceptionally large area of ancient woodland containing more than 1,000 ancient trees. A deeply incised narrow valley with combes, it is a dramatic landform near the north coast of Exmoor and the open moorland of Dunkery. It is an excellent example of a temperate rainforest.

Designations:

Dunkery and Horner Wood NNR (1626ha)
Exmoor and Quantock oak woodlands SAC
North Exmoor SSSI
National Trust ownership.

Issue:

Despite being part of the Dunkery and Horner National Nature Reserve (NNR), one of the largest terrestrial NNRs in England and the first within Exmoor, Horner Wood is being increasingly used and promoted as an area for play and 'adventure'. Nature and landscape conservation should be the overriding management objective of all NNRs, as agreed in this case when it was declared in 1995, and this should take precedence over other objectives such as access.

Impact on:

Landscape beauty, and tranquillity

The wood is used extensively by local dog walkers, sometimes in large groups, often resulting in unwelcome noise from barking dogs, loss of tranquillity along the valley bottom near the river and a proliferation of 'poo' bags. The use of the steep paths and tracks by mountain bikers has increased dramatically over the last 10 years, leading to excessive noise, erosion and conflict with other users. Bike events occur frequently, where large numbers of riders descend from Dunkery downhill to the Vale at high speed.

Wildlife

The wood is extremely rich in wildlife, a prime site for migratory birds such as redstarts and hugely important for bats – Horner is used by 16 of the 17 UK breeding species. When the NNR management plan was originally drawn up, it was agreed that the east bank of Horner Water (up to the East Water junction) should be inaccessible to people. This is no longer the case and the whole valley floor is now used by people and dogs. The wildlife is threatened by this and there is even disturbance at night with regular excursions by groups of bikers, using bright lights.

Archaeology/Cultural Heritage

Horner Wood is rich in archaeological sites with 54 sites/ha, compared to 14/ha on the open moorland. The large number of charcoal platforms, the Tudor iron smelting works and the medieval village site on the slopes below Ley Hill are at risk from potential or real damage from mountain bikes and increased numbers of people.

Options:

- Visitors (local and tourists) understand that they are in a sensitive, special place – an NNR.
- Visitor management to reduce the impact of footfall, dogs and mountain bike activities
- Make nature the first management priority – reroute public access to reduce disturbance and minimise impact

Recommendations:

- Positive promotion of the NNR to highlight its nature conservation objectives
- Avoid any commercial activity events within the wood
- Improve local signage and information to explain more about the importance of this rare asset.

Exmoor Society Sensitive Sites Assessment form

May Bank Holiday Landacre (ENPA)

At Landacre, Jo Down, whose family have owned the land on Withypool Common and Sherdon since 1977, has noticed a huge increase in visitors and more importantly a change in the way they behave. The Barle and Sherdon Water meet just above Landacre bridge forming a deep pool, the river is clear running over small pebbles and stone and the banks, grazed short, are perfect for a picnic. It is open and sunny, there is parking, and it is beautiful. "What more," Jo asks, "could people want?" And that is the difficulty, because the answer is not much, so they come, in their hundreds.

Last year people came most days and on high days and holidays there were on average 50-100 cars or about 100-300 people a day and some stayed to party and camp at night. Often, they were first time visitors who haven't yet developed a relationship to Exmoor. National Park rangers pick up bags of rubbish but Jo fantasises about them leaving it in a vast mound so that visitors can see the damage that is being done. What worries her more though is the less visible impact on the river. The few miles upstream of Landacre is the main spawning ground for endangered Atlantic Salmon for the entire River Exe system. As the salmon head up from the coast in the first spate they search for a quiet pool where, tired and hungry, they wait until December when they spawn. Or perhaps just until a joyful dog leaps in after a stick. Or a kayak crashes, or a swimmer splashes past. The use of spot-on flea and tick treatments that comes off dogs as they play in the river is another huge concern as this devastates the invertebrates.

"The question is what can be done? Physical barriers are an option – gates, fences, boulders in laybys."

The question is what can be done? Physical barriers are an option – gates, fences, boulders in lay-bys. In Simonsbath, the parish have used large stones to stop parking on the road. Jo Down has put a gate across her track to Sherdon Hutch and posts block cars getting onto the river bank. There could be signs, bins, and ropes – the

Landacre (Jo Minoprio)

paraphernalia of urban parks. A licensing scheme could be introduced for big sporting events. There could also be a legal response. Although privately owned, as with much of Exmoor, the land around Landacre is both in the National Park and Open Access and a common misapprehension is that this means visitors are free to go and do whatever takes their fancy. The law, however, is restrictive. There is no right to drive and camp off road, set fires and leave litter. According to Natural England these all contravene both the CROW (Countryside Rights of Way) and the Wildlife and Countryside Act – but exactly who might be responsible or

> "… on Exmoor there are thirteen SSSIs, three NNRs and 2 SACs, constituting 28% of the park."

willing to enforce the law is unclear. In some of the other National Parks it is different but Jo Down says that she feels let down by the lack of support from either Natural England or the National Park, and the police on Exmoor have bigger fish to fry than chasing campers and off-roaders round the moor.

A longer-term response would be behavioural change. In a presentation to the Campaign for National Parks, the environmentalist Katherine Clarke[3] used her training in behavioural science to describe the ways in which people respond to being in nature. What emerges is a clash between those who, usually from childhood, have developed the knowledge, beliefs and values that make them behave in ways that protect nature and those who haven't. In almost all cases,

unless a site is specifically set up for visitors, there are difficulties at beauty spots that leave the 'protectors' baffled and resentful. She often hears, 'it's unbelievable,' and 'they should…'. But people, she argues, are inevitable and need to be considered as part of the system from the start. The challenge is to get more of them on the 'protect' side and to achieve this the knowledge, beliefs and values that threaten nature need to be changed.

Knowledge is in some ways the easiest. It comes from education and information but also from experience and watching others. Example creates permission so if dogs are off leads, people are barbecuing, camping, swimming and leaving litter then this becomes the norm. Beliefs are less tangible and emerge from the outcomes of experience or what one has seen or heard from others. They can conflict as in the belief that a dog needs to run free to get enough exercise and the belief that they may then disturb wildlife. Beliefs then get referred to values which is where it gets tricky – what does one value more the dog or the birds? A swim or the salmon? This is where the gap between intention and behaviour opens up and it is in this muddy, conflicted chasm that interventions need to occur. These can be barriers and they can be aids – more knowledge informing different habits, creating new social norms and so, hey presto, no litter, no fires and no dogs chasing after balls, sheep or anything else.

The International Union for the Conservation of Nature (IUCN) has six categories for protected areas and England's national parks come way down the list at 5, designated as Protected Landscapes. This categorises areas whose character has been created by the interaction of people and nature over time and, unlike IUCN Nature Reserves,

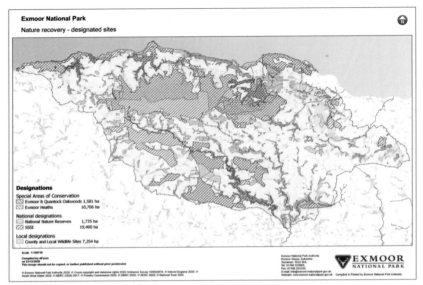

Nature Recovery, Designated Areas

they are not managed for wilderness. Rather they are working landscapes and from their inception there to be understood and enjoyed by visitors. But they are also some of the last bastions of beauty and reservoirs of nature in the country. On Exmoor there are thirteen SSSIs, three NNRs and 2 SACs, constituting 28% of the park. They overlap and of the SSSIs surveyed by Natural England over the last ten years, 80% were judged 'unfavourable, improving'. It is extraordinarily difficult to reconcile the competing needs of people and nature, it is not a new problem and nor is it one that is going to go away. But if the protection of 'special habitats and species' (SAC), 'important habitats, species, geology' (NNR) 'wildlife, fauna, geology or landform of special interest' (SSSI) is to mean anything perhaps, at least in these precious fragments, natural beauty and non-human needs should take priority. As Lord Sandford wrote way back in 1974:

National Park Authorities can do much to reconcile public enjoyment with the preservation of natural beauty by good planning and management and the main emphasis must continue to be on this approach wherever possible. But even so, there will be situations where the two purposes are irreconcilable... Where this happens, priority must be given to the conservation of natural beauty. [4]

But even if priority is given to nature, the question remains: who is going to have the money, the means and the mandate to protect it? ◆

1   DEFRA – Landscapes Review – Final Report 2019, p.16
2   https://www.gov.uk/check-your-business-protected-area
3   Katherine Clarke, Bee Kinder
4   Sandford, Lord (1974). Report of the National Parks Policy Review Committee. (Sandford Report). London: HMSO.

MOOR LIFE

EXFORD 2¼

CLOUTSHAM 2½

STOKE PERO 2

PORLOCK POST

POSTCARD FROM THE PAST

This picture of Minehead Beach was taken in the late 1930s. In 1939, just before the outbreak of World War II, a touring circus took elephants to seaside resorts all round the West Country – and they probably travelled by train. It gives rewilding a whole new meaning.

THE VIEW FROM THE PARK

Sarah Bryan
Chief Executive of the ENPA

After such a turbulent year, you may be surprised to hear that there has been any silver lining at all. But the way staff, businesses and local communities have pulled together, to adapt to new ways of working and ultimately make our places safe and accessible again, has been nothing short of inspirational. It's this sheer resilience that is testament to all those who care about the moor and that, I believe, captures the true spirit of Exmoor.

A key impact of the pandemic has been to create major fluctuations in the public's use of our rights of way network. Paths of

"... the way staff, businesses and local communities have pulled together, to adapt to new ways of working and ultimately make our places safe and accessible again, has been nothing short of inspirational."

National Park Centre, Dunster

Statutory Meetings online (ENPA)

all sorts proved even more vital to people's health and wellbeing to exercise and escape the unfolding tragedy. In the lockdowns it was mainly residents out using the paths, which kept footfall largely localised around villages and settlements. But this pattern quickly shifted as people flocked from the surrounding areas upon the easing of travel restrictions.

Some were old friends and others new to Exmoor but all were seeking the same sense of freedom and solace, and it was here they chose to escape after months of isolation in their own gardens and well-trodden local green spaces. Even more shocking was the 1 in 8 people who, according to ONS figures, spent the lockdowns without any access to a garden at all.

For our access teams (as well as our wildlife), the flux in visitors represented a real challenge. They switched to emergency only response on maintenance and instead spent time establishing systems to aid social distancing and hygiene. Rangers also played a key role in supporting landowners with rights of way issues, and they helped to deliver food and medical supplies to remote communities as part of Devon and Somerset's coordinated pandemic emergency response.

Meanwhile all staff at our National Park Centres and head offices moved to remote working. Being able to adapt meant many staff and Members working outside their field of experience to upskill and overhaul systems, and I'm grateful to all of them for their flexibility and determination – a rapid learning curve for all of us given the trials of on-line meetings.

Despite all this, our service delivery barely skipped a beat, with the first of our virtual Authority meetings taking place on 14th May last year with only one month forgone. As a result, our planning department was able to continue to recover following robust action to deal with a temporary drop in performance. Thanks to a decisive move to boost capacity, planning targets continued to improve despite the pandemic and are now back to exceeding national targets.

Last year also proved to be our most successful year to date in terms of rights of way maintenance, with an impressive 98% of paths logged as open and easy to use in our annual survey. A remarkable feat when you consider the increased

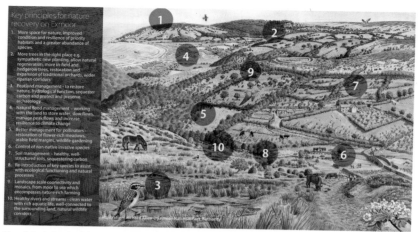

Key Principles for Nature Recovery on Exmoor (ENPA)

public footfall that continued throughout peak tourism season, alongside the impact of self-isolation, sickness and school closures on staff and volunteer capacity.

It goes without saying that our economy has been hard hit by the pandemic and, in particular, the tourism and hospitality sectors that make up two thirds of employment on Exmoor. We mobilised a responsive network of tourism partners to lead a united Exmoor Tourism Recovery Plan which was widely acclaimed and has since been held up nationally as an example of best practice.

As confidence grew within these new socially-distanced ways of working, so too did our ability to move beyond the pandemic and resume delivering across more of our corporate goals, achieving some truly remarkable results for the year. These included:

- The reinstatement of Woodside Bridge
- Exmoor's first ever Nature Recovery Vision adopted last autumn
- The Defra Test and Trial project completed, involving 26 land holdings across Exmoor

- New assets for Astrotourism
- The completion of a survey of Exmoor's existing economy
- More boots on the ground with new assistant and seasonal ranger posts established
- The first few hundred saplings planted towards the creation of Bye Wood
- 18 new affordable homes built in Dulverton and the six local need one-bed homes all occupied
- Virtual volunteering
- Pinkery Centre for Outdoor learning received an interior makeover

This is by no means an exhaustive list but I hope it gives you a flavour of some of the achievements made during this most challenging of years. None of this would be possible without the incredible adaptability and resolve shared by all those who know and love Exmoor and I look forward to working with you all again as we move forward with the pandemic and put into practice some of the unexpected learning and skills many of us have gained along the way. ◆

(Anjelica Tarnowska)

THE DAILY MORNING MIRACLE

So I put on my pants and stump outside. *It's true –*
the light is back – dim in the holly copse,
blinking in colours on crackled stubble-tops
by Hoar Oak Batch, and pale in furrows through

Beet Field, like spilled white paint. Three cut-out magpies
stare at the sky from Tidball's foggy gate;
violet-pated turnips peer from a crate.
The world has sprung its daily, grand surprise.

I hurry, amazed, down Teazel Lane, where
the dazzled thornheads and a single daffodil
punctuate the morning miracle
with exclamations in the brightening air.

I walk the turning world to Ruddock Rise.
Six-Spots reel the furze; the sudden season
seems to reach perfection without reason;
As earth rolls out its daily, grand surprise.

John Gallas

REVIEWS, ARTS AND CRAFTS

BOOKS

RETHINKING FOOD AND AGRICULTURE: NEW WAYS FORWARD

eds. Amir Kassam and Laila Kassam (2021)
Woodhead Publishing, Cambridge (Elsevier)
Paperback, 476 pages, £165
Paperback ISBN: 9780128164105
(eBook ISBN: 9780128164112)

This timely, thoroughly referenced book proposes system-wide changes to international food and agriculture. Revised policies are perceived as vital if globally sustainable agriculture and improved environmental management are to be achieved. It highlights the progressive loss of biodiversity, especially since 1950, together with extensive land degradation, reduced climate resilience and eroded sovereignty for local food systems and farming communities. It clearly documents the collision between industrialised, intensive, transnational agribusiness on the one hand and the agro-ecological, biodiverse, sustainable, resilient, family farming systems that are pursued by the majority of the world's farmers on the other (including those larger-scale farmers who value the managerial sovereignty of farmers). The impressive breadth of its research shows unequivocally that despite the scandal of there being almost 1 billion hungry people on earth, there is enough food to feed far more than the present population of (almost) 8 billion. This counters the frequent argument that there is a need to expand productivity; an argument used to justify as 'inevitable' further industrialisation of agriculture, including the increased use of genetically modified (GM) technologies.

This new book does not merely criticise contemporary food and agriculture, it offers real evidence of how to improve farming and food systems. However, it might be seen to over-emphasise veganism, which it sets against all livestock farming. There is a consensus that human beings need to consume a higher proportion of plants for both agricultural system efficiency and healthier diets. However, a future edition could properly include a chapter on attempts to improve grassland and rangeland farming systems as advocated by the Pasture-fed Livestock Association (https://www.pfla.org).

The opening chapter by Rupert Sheldrake, *Setting innovation free in agriculture,* is a *tour de force,* and the book goes on to discuss a wide range of ideas and issues with each of its 20 chapters written by a different author and expert.

Chapter 2 blames agriculture for planting the seeds of alienation from nature, arguing that the misinterpretation of 'dominion' (Genesis 1: 26-28) has been used to justify 'dominionism'. The theological perspective is a welcome inclusion in the debate about agriculture's future but context is needed for it to be relevant. Furthermore, 'misothery', Jim Mason's term for the contempt of animals and nature, does not characterise attitudes of the vast majority of farmers engaged in caring animal husbandry, any more than does atheism.

In Chapter 7, Tony Juniper cogently presents the improvements that will lead to a sustainable food system, strongly endorsed by Hans Herren who stresses the need for an agro-ecological approach. We are omnivores, as Colin Tudge wisely points out in his excellent Chapter 9, with mixed farming systems offering real hope for the future. Internationally distinguished Amir Kassam, writing on *Paradigms of Agriculture,* provides a well-supported endorsement of Conservation Agriculture and its associated soil health improvements.

Allison Wilson of BRP Ithaca USA, asks *Will gene-edited and other GM crops fail sustainable food systems?* She offers a brilliant and balanced critique of GM/nGM technologies and their performance to date, together with the already known catalogue of unintended consequences. It should be read by all government policymakers and anyone still convinced

by the prospects of GM in agriculture.

In Chapter 15 on *Healthy Diets as a Guide to Responsible Food Systems,* Shireen Kassam *et al* present a clear case for diets centred on unprocessed whole plant food, and the need for change in vested interests for that to occur. With his characteristic wisdom, Robert Chambers, brother of Jackie Edwards of Westermill Farm Exford, goes on to reflect on the importance of *Knowledge Systems for inclusively responsible food and agriculture.* He affirms the importance of putting farmers, their communities and natural resources first.

Chapter 19 by Vandana Shiva superbly summarises *Co-creating responsible food and agriculture systems* ,from 'the path of death to the path of life'. She passionately concludes: "Real food with integrity comes from real farmers with integrity working with the integrity of the Earth and ecological processes…when we participate in living economies that regenerate the well-being of all, we sow the seeds of our future".

In their conclusion, *Toward Inclusive Responsibility,* the editors face the daunting task of trying to draw together a wealth of material. For this reviewer, their attempt to conflate proven conservation agriculture with veganism is a real pity: **Conservation Agriculture-based Veganic Agroecology**, while being a great debate-starter, is not exactly a rallying cry for the urgently needed championing of **agroecology**.

John Wibberley

ENTANGLED LIFE: HOW FUNGI MAKE OUR WORLDS, CHANGE OUR MINDS AND SHAPE OUR FUTURES

Merlin Sheldrake
Hb, 356 pp, The Bodley Head, £20.00
ISBN: 978 184 792 5190

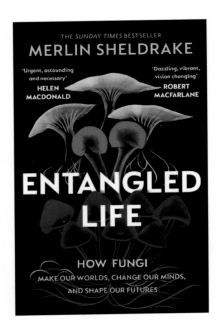

Custodian of curious minds will doubtless be enthralled by the entangled hyphae of fungal facts, tantalising tales and grotesque goings-on which Dr Merlin Sheldrake presents for our delectation and amazement in this glorious tome dedicated to the biology, history and ambition of the humble fungi. Enigmatic chapter titles (Living Labyrinths, Mycelial Minds, Wood Wide Webs) invite you into this cordial realm of approachable information, wonder and delight. The referencing is comprehensive and stated with accuracy and integrity. There are colour photos as well as reproductions of illustrations created with the ink of the Shaggy Inkcap… and there are a few long words (but don't worry too much about those).

The name of Merlin Sheldrake made its literary debut in Robert Macfarlane's 2019 epic, *Underland: A deep time journey* when 'the young plant scientist' helped to explain the mysteries of The Understorey in Epping Forest. Since then, Sheldrake has travelled the world in pursuit of mycological knowledge and experiences in his passionate quest to fairly place the hitherto misunderstood (and somewhat maligned) Kingdom of Fungi, within the global ecological framework and show how important it is to the ongoing discourse on climate, carbon release and storage, renewable energy sources, sustainable manufacturing processes, food production and habitat conservation. As reward for his investigations and revelations, it seems likely that *Entangled Life* will join *Underland* on bookshelves

across the world for a long time to come.

'Whether in forests, labs or kitchens, fungi have changed my understanding of how life happens.' So says Sheldrake, and he goes much, much further in his explanations and descriptions, uncovering the alchemy of fungal existence and illuminating its effect upon us all – whether we yet realise it, or not. Fungi as fermenters, brewers; fungi as tangy blue cheese delicacies: fungi as aromatic, extortionately expensive truffles; fungi as medicine; fungi as superfoods. Fungi as information networks; fungi as controllers of animal behaviour: fungi as facilitators of plant nutrition. Fungi as furniture; fungi as shoes; fungi as houses. Fungi as destroyers; fungi as recyclers; fungi in your compost heap, decaying your lawn clippings, heating up your leafmould, releasing carbon compounds into the Exmoor climate. Lichens and fungi created the Exmoor landscape and now another fungus, Hymenoscyphus fraxineus, is changing it as Ash Dieback disease alters the future of Exmoor.

Entangled Life: How fungi make our worlds, change our minds and shape our futures is a book for anyone interested in ecology, the natural world, biology, cooking, engineering, medicine, psychology, entomology, brewing, travel, music, poetry, literature, mathematics, neuroscience, fashion, spiritual life, manufacturing, space exploration, research & development technology, physiology, biocomputing, dogs… In fact, if you draw breath, wear clothes and think that life is not too short to stuff a mushroom, there's a likelihood that this book is for you. Prepare to be astounded and enjoy the ride.

Siân Parry, Fungi Recorder for Exmoor Natural History Society www.enhs.org.uk

---

BEES IN MY BONNET

Julian Willford
Wire Books, Warmington,
Oxfordshire,2021
Paperback, 160 pages, £10
Pb ISBN: 978-0-9933464-1-5

Exmoor farmer Julian Willford's sweeping account of his life is a farming and spiritual odyssey. It is a journey that starts in New Zealand and ends in Africa – by way of farming in Herefordshire, Wales and latterly Exmoor.

Julian and wife Zoe farmed in south-west Wales before purchasing Allercot, a 220-acre Exmoor farm in 1982. He describes how, when they turned off the road near Couple Cross and went down the hill to the farm, it was 'love at first sight'. Its previous owner was looking for someone who would 'fit in locally and look after the land properly' and Julian and Zoe seemed to fit the bill.

Starting from scratch, they purchased livestock from local auctions and grew their flock. His account reflects the huge challenge of making enough income on a relatively small hill farm, when much of the land is woodland and the rest rough grazing. From music festivals and field archery to motocross and horse carriage driving, the book romps through his efforts to supplement traditional Exmoor farming with new ventures, more or less successful. A struggle that will resonate with many readers.

Wherever he roamed though, Julian never left behind his bees. They are his great passion and when not on Exmoor he buzzes off to Africa and helps Bees Abroad, a global charity that develops beekeeping in some of the world's poorest countries. His skills as a beekeeper have benefited many African countries as a result and he tells vivid tales of encounters with African Honeybees – more aggressive and challenging to work with than their Exmoor cousins.

Much of the book traces Julian's spiritual journey; from his discovery of Transcendental Meditation in India to the visit from the Holy Spirit that gave the pastor a shock in Minehead. And the retreats and meditation courses he held in the beautiful surroundings of Allercott that were one of his more unusual 'farm diversifications'. This is an entertaining and thoughtful story of a life packed with adventure.

Lisa Eden

PARRACOMBE PRIZE 2020

Available from admin@parracombe.org.uk

When lockdown brought rural life to a halt the people of Parracombe found a new way to pass the time. Already engaged in a major fundraising campaign to build a community shop and repair an ageing village hall, Parracombe Community Trust needed innovative ideas to raise additional cash. The village's book group answered the call by launching a short story competition. Initially, the aim was to raise money while challenging North Devon residents to fill their empty hours, but thanks to social media word spread and the *Parracombe Prize 2020* received nearly 400 entries from all over the world. Entrants paid £5, and each story was read at least three times by a panel before the winners of the prizes were decided.

The result is a 60,000-word anthology containing 35 original stories, now being sold to fill Parracombe's coffers. It includes a story by North Devon writer, Simon Dawson, who spoke for many

when he said: 'A national lockdown, and all its solitude, proved a perfect time to write. For me, supporting a great cause by doing something I enjoy was a great way to pass time.'

A MAP OF LYNTON AND LYNMOUTH IN 1840

Martin Ebdon

Ebdon, M.,2021, *Sheet 3 of the Devon in 1840 Series*
ISBN 978-0-9930072-4-8

This series of exquisite maps, published by Martin Ebdon, are based on the tithe surveys of 1840. Their aim is to construct general purpose maps of the landscape as it was in the early years of the reign of Queen Victoria. This year, A Map of Lynton and Lynmouth joins the series and provides an extraordinary insight into both how much north Devon has changed and how much has stayed the same. Two drawings of Lynton by George Rowe printed on the back give an even greater idea of the beauty of the town in the mid nineteenth century.

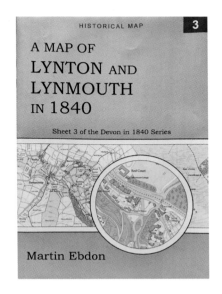

HISTORICAL MAP   3

A MAP OF
LYNTON AND
LYNMOUTH
IN 1840

Sheet 3 of the Devon in 1840 Series

Martin Ebdon

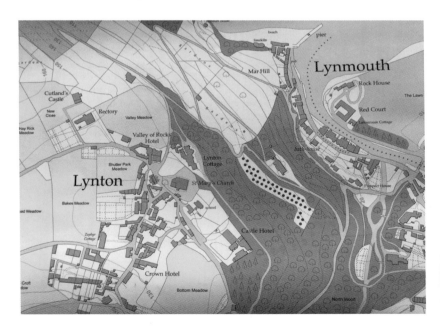

AN INDEX TO THE EXMOOR REVIEW

The first copy of the *Exmoor Review* was produced in 1959, a year after the Society was founded, priced one shilling and sixpence. Since then, there has been an *Exmoor Review* every year, except for 1964 and 1965 which is covered by a single issue (something that can cause significant confusion for somebody compiling an index!). One of the fantastic things about the *Review* is that it contains a record of reflections, from a wide variety of informed and passionate people, about such a unique area. Local people, policymakers, academics, and others who wouldn't want to be labelled, have left a legacy that charts Exmoor's ups and downs for over 60 years. It is important that their insight and wisdom are available to as broad an audience as possible.

We have become so used to obtaining information at the press of a button. One of the problems with the *Review* is that historic copies are not available in a "searchable" format thus an index is useful. This year I finally brought the index for the *Review* up to date. This builds on the work of Victor Bonham-Carter and Dr Glynn Court who produced an index to the first 35 issues. I have reworked this and added the contents of a further 27 issues. We now have an index that covers 2,659 articles,

Exmoor Review No 1

references 2,736 authors, and has articles listed under multiple subject headings (5,753 in total).

It is currently available as a spreadsheet. I am intending to also produce a hardcopy. It will be updated each year with the articles from the latest addition. It has been hard work to compile, but it has also been a joy. I have had the opportunity to engage with the work of so many interesting people and I hope that this complete index will make the work of all those who contribute to the *Review* more widely available.

Sean Beer

ART

THE ARBOREALISTS

New woodlands in the National Park are being supported by an exhibition of work by the Arborealists, an acclaimed group of artists who share a passion for trees. Formed in 2013, the Arborealists are the brain child of curator and artist Tim Craven and their works have been shown all over the country but this is their first show on Exmoor. Organised by local artist Jo Minoprio in partnership with Exmoor National Park Authority, the 16-day exhibition will be held at Lanacre Barn Gallery, Withypool in November with donations and a percentage of sales going towards the planting of Bye Wood outside Winsford.

Turkey tail fungus (Mike Dodd, Arborealists)

Tamsin Waley-Cohen

MUSIC

THE TWO MOORS FESTIVAL

Two weekends of music on Dartmoor and Exmoor in October allow the new artistic director of the Two Moors Festival, the violinist Tamsin Waley-Cohen, to celebrate wilderness and the rediscovery of the world outside our doors. The festival was founded by John and Penny Adie as a response to the Foot and Mouth crisis of 2001 which was devastating to the area, and its extraordinary quality continues to provide succour in difficult times.

Following largely online concerts, Waley-Cohen curated her first full festival in an area to which she is strongly connected. The theme and title were Arcadia Unlocked. It was a celebration of the Natural World that has proved so important.

FOOD

'GRANNY'S BUTTER APPLE CRUMBLE'

Last year *Rachel Johnson* reached the finals of BBC1's Celebrity Home Cook – this is the recipe that got her there.

Granny could only make two things but, like the hedgehog, she did both very well. The first was a cold rice salad with tomato, onion and tuna, the second was her crumble that she would let us help her with in the kitchen at Nethercote, accompanied by her terriers who supplemented their diet with her rubbery hearing aids. Must be made with Bramleys or another cooking apple – nothing mushy or tasteless! My only life skill is the ability – learned on her knee as a small child – to make a crumble in five minutes flat.

3-4 cooking apples (Bramleys)
Half a pack of butter and more for apples and top
Lemon rind and juice
6oz Flour
3oz Soft Dark Brown Sugar
(All measurements approx. as I never measure anything)

Core and finely chop the unpeeled Bramleys and place in the bottom of a large greased baking dish. Sprinkle with sugar, lemon rind slivers, lemon juice, a splash of water and dot with butter, and stick in the oven on about 150 while you make the crumble in a bowl with the flour, sugar and butter. Pour the rubble onto the apple (if not enough, make more, you can never have too much crumble), dot with more butter, and bake until brown on top and dark-bubbly round the edges.

Rose wickwar

PLANTS

ROSE WICKWAR

Mark Luytens chooses his perfect Exmoor plant

Rose Wickwar looks good on Exmoor and does well – it also seems to be sheep-proof! Peter Beales lists it as a 'medium sized' shrub up to 3 metres; in my experience, it does twice that up into a tree or hedge where it can grow freely. In my opinion, the key to gardening on Exmoor is to chose those plants that thrive and to plant them in sufficient numbers so that they look as if they are growing naturally, to blur the edges between the garden and the wider landscape. Exmoor is predominantly deciduous, exuberant and, in flower, white; Wickwar ticks all those boxes.

I first saw it in a nursery in Gloucestershire near to the place – Wickwar – where it was discovered growing by the nurseryman Keith Steadman. It's a Himalayan rose, similar to Kiftsgate but, arguably, easier to live with. When I saw it, it was growing over an old stump by the front gate, a great mound of blue-green leaf and masses of single white flowers with yellow centres – it was the most beautiful sight, enough to make me drive in and ask what it was.

6 months later, I was given a small rooted cutting. It looked unprepossessing but I was assured that it would grow – and it did. Since then, I have taken a number of cuttings and planted them in the hedges around the edges of the garden where, in July, it is spectacular. It needs space and should be kept away from paths as it's a brute, with many, very sharp thorns which snag and tear anything within reach of its long, arching branches. In autumn, it has orange hips.

OBITUARIES

WILLIAM GEORGE WITHERIDGE

George was born on the 11th June 1942 the second of three children, belonging to Jack and Hilda Witheridge who farmed East Bushton as tenants of the Fortescue Estate. In 1944 the family were offered the tenancy of Middle Stoodleigh where they remain to this day, buying the farm when the Fortescue Estate sold the western side in 1960.

George was educated at West Buckland Village School and then West Buckland where he was a day boy at Fortescue House. But he was always absorbed by the farm and when he was 16 left to help his father. Back at Middle Stoodleigh he missed the company of the like-minded farmers' sons he had met at school so joined Swimbridge YFC, in time becoming its chairman and in the mid 1960s, group chairman of the Barnstaple Federation of YFC. It was while involved with Swimbridge YFC that he got to know Pat Balment and in1965 they married and had their two children, John born in 1968 and Sarah in 1972.

Midst all of this activity, George's goals were not yet fulfilled. He learnt to shear and he pursued the skills of the farrier. This reduced his outgoings over time and in 1968, under the tutelage of Les Dayment, he became an Associate of the Worshipful Company of Farriers. Such was the stature of the man that his help was sought on a wider front in the community of West Buckland village and he served on the Parish Council for many years. He was also on the village hall committee and was involved when it was extended to become a very attractive and now much used village hall. He also took care of the worshipping community at

George Witheridge

St Peter's Church where he served as Church Warden for 30 years.

When you think of all that was going on in George's life between family, work and community, you could be forgiven for posing the question 'when did he ever relax?' Of course the answer was when he was astride one of his hunters with the Devon and Somerset Staghounds in whose country he lived and with whom the family has had a lifelong association managing the red deer population. In the 1953 season, when George was in his first year at West Buckland, he and his father Jack are named as part of the harbouring team covering the country. Nine years later, in the 1962 season, they were gun carriers. With these opportunities to watch the deer and study their habits and follow the hounds on hunting days, there was barely any place in the country that George did not know. This made him a terrific guide and mentor to many; his memory was such that he could remember runs, how and where the deer had been found, the route it had travelled and eventually where it had been taken. In all this he was a very faithful and helpful member of the Hunt Committee.

In 1995 George and Pat joined forces to assist with the running of Exford Show, Pat as secretary and George as a Vice president and, helped by their family and others, they did this faithfully until they retired in in 2017. In 1998 George, described 'as an affable and well respected Staghunter, from the Barnstaple Side' became even more important to the hunt when he was invited to share the Field Mastership with John Blackband. By the 2000 season he had joined Maurice and Diana Scott in the Mastership. Unfortunately, he had to have both hips done in 2007 and finally called time in 2011, after a nasty fall on the road at Heasley Mill.

George joined the mastership in the days of the political struggle that embroiled hunting at the turn of the century and the ban in 2004. He also saw the door reopen with permission for deer management. It meant that he never really stopped and even after his accident with the help of two kind friends, Peter Turner and John Burrough, he got out hunting – even if it was on four wheels rather than four legs.

Unfortunately, lockdown played a sad part and the isolation and lack of interests of the last year saw George's health decline. On the evening of the 2nd June Toby his faithful steed, now aged 29, was brought down to the bungalow and from his sick bed George, without a word, gave him the thumbs-up. Later that night, on the 3rd June 2021, he quietly passed away.

Ron Smith

GILL LANGDON

Gill and her family came to Exmoor on their holidays from Southend, where her father practised as a GP. They then settled at Bullseye, Luckwell Bridge, in the heart of Exmoor National Park. Gill trained as a Radiologist and was based at Minehead hospital until her retirement at the age of 60. She and Roly Langdon married late in life; they had been secretly engaged for many years, as she cared for her disabled parents till their deaths.

The Exmoor Pony Society was a great passion and she and her sister Jackie started the Tawbits herd. Watching tiny Gill wrestling a rough stallion, just off the moor, was a sight to see! The two sisters endlessly supported the Society and the Minehead Harriers; raising funds at every opportunity. Chutneys, jams, cakes, sausage rolls, soups and full breakfasts came in an endless stream from their kitchen and ever expanding freezer.

The other part of Gill's life was wrapped up in the Church and everything to do with it. The Primary school and preschool of Cutcombe saw her every week and generations of children knew Gill from a very early age; then brought their children to the school to learn the story of Jesus from her. On Palm Sunday Gill would bring a donkey and lead the procession from the school to the Church, though to some it appeared that the donkey was leading her. Gill also led the Benefice Mother's Union which raised funds and met once a month.

The Harvest Supper was always a huge success. The children would bring fruit and vegetables to Gill who would auction them after the sumptuous Harvest Supper meal laid on by the village ladies – always with Gill darting around, making sure everything was done. At Christingle, Jackie and Gill would give all the children and teenagers the traditional orange adorned with sweets and symbols of Christian life. Gill was a stalwart member of the Exmoor Benefice choir. This was her relaxation and playtime and she cherished the weekly hour of rehearsals, giggling at mistakes and having a good time with her friends.

At the heart of Cutcombe Church for many years Gill was a very faithful Churchwarden. Nothing escaped her attention, from laundering the Altar Cloth to providing the wine for communion. When the Church building was closed for restoration, services were held at the Village Hall and Gill would turn the Hall into a place of Worship. Again, when the pandemic struck, the Church building was closed for a time but Gill made sure it was open as soon as Government legislation allowed: first for private prayer two hours a day for anyone who wished to slip in and then for regular services.

Eccentricity is quite normal on Exmoor and Gill lived up to the motto 'throw nothing away' so, to the very end, she wore suits she'd made for her mother in the 60's and reindeer boots with turned up toes. Gill and Jackie made food for the Village Fête and then bought everything left at the auction which would go into the vast freezer.

The hole Gill has left in our church, village and pony loving communities is huge, a lasting testament to a tiny person who gave us all so much. A woman of strong faith Gill died in the sure hope of the Resurrection which she had done so much to bring to others in her life.

Mully Woolmer

Gill at Exford Show in 1973 with Hawkwell Lady Margaret as a three year-old. Margaret was Gill's foundation mare for the Tawbitts herd

BETTYE NELDER

For thirty years pupils at Dulverton Middle School knew when Mrs Nelder was coming – they were always warned by the clippity clop of the high heels she wore to work on the hard wooden floors.

Secretary to the school; leader for the Beavers and Guides in Dulverton, Brushford and Bampton; volunteer for TicVac, a charity that helped disabled children during the holidays and President of the Tiverton Siroptomist volunteer movement that works to support women and girls across the globe – Bettye's great love was children and she devoted her life to her own and others.

Born in Harrow in 1934, Bettye was Betty Austin then. After school she trained at secretarial college and then worked in the City at a bank and an Estate Agents in Wealdstone, which is where she met Chris. They married in 1957 and moved back to Dulverton where Chris's family worked in the Carnarvon Arms garage in Brushford. Her three children, Garry, Suzanne and Christine were born soon after and looking for something to do with them she used her great energy to help set up a toddler group. When the children were old enough she returned to full time work at what was then Dulverton Secondary Modern School, where, as school secretary, she comforted generations of children with grazed knees and other sorrows.

When she wasn't organising the school, she was organizing the family – the children, the grandchildren, the great grandchildren. The series of houses they lived in were always spick and span including the last, 41 Northmoor Road, which she particularly loved. Her other love was cars. When the children were young, ever loyal, Bettye would bring one of the girls along to watch Chris banger racing and always bring a picnic. Once they left, she began to enjoy old cars in her own right, particularly Mary Jane, a 1933 Austin 12. She and Chris formed the affiliated Somerset Austin Club and, together with Mary Jane, spent many happy days travelling all over England and beyond.

Bettye Nelder died 7th June 2020 in Northmoor Road in Dulverton above the family's bakery.

Chris Nelder

2021 PINNACLE AWARD WINNER
Caroline Westcott

Who would start a business, get it going full tilt and aim it at a brick wall? And who would hit the wall, come out the other side and keep going? Some of Exmoor's young people have being doing just this, and I take my hat off to them. These are the people by whom Exmoor will stand or fall. Without them our communities will fade, and the life of the moor will disappear, leaving only its picture-postcard setting.

I've just seen the publicly available data for the majority of Exmoor, and it shows what you would expect – the majority of the population without dependent children is doing very nicely thank you, but the opposite is true for families. Things got markedly worse between 2015 and 2019, and that was before COVID.

"Making sure there are opportunities for the working age population is the crucial challenge for everyone who loves Exmoor and the Pinnacle Award is the Exmoor Society's response."

Making sure there are opportunities for the working age population is the crucial challenge for everyone who loves Exmoor and the Pinnacle Award is the Exmoor Society's response. Its purpose is to

"Its purpose is to encourage young people whose aspiration and ambition is to make their lives here."

encourage young people whose aspiration and ambition is to make their lives here – good and satisfying lives – and make an essential contribution to Exmoor's economy and the wellbeing of our common life. The injection of capital it gives makes a real difference.

This year's winner is Caroline Westcott who, not having the benefit of second sight, launched her business, with great success, straight at the COVID wall. She has survived the crash, used the hiatus to think through longer-term plans and, as lockdown eases, she is busier by the day

School at West Buckland fostered her interest in cooking, and the idea that going away from Exmoor should be part of her life. So, she went to Cirencester to train as a property agent, and then on to London. She knew if she didn't go, she'd always wonder what she'd missed but she also knew that she would come back. Her life would be here.

All the while she was cooking for friends, entertaining, experimenting and developing her skills and ideas. Cooking is what she loves best. She didn't abandon Exmoor in her London years, so of course her skill was known here just as much as there. Some travelling followed, and it gave her the perspective and time to plan a business that would allow her to live on the moor, and would play to her skills and her love.

Caroline's food was already well known on Exmoor and in 2018 she got the chance to take on the shoot lunches at Chargot for the season. This would be a step up, so she went to Ashburton Chefs Academy for a month's intensive training to make sure she succeeded as she took on something much bigger than she had ever done.

The season was a triumph. Now for summer work. Judicious use of social media reached her own generation and, for others, her address book. She had large postcards printed to show her dishes and, importantly, a photograph of herself on the other side. Hundreds of hand-addressed envelopes later

"She had large postcards printed to show her dishes and, importantly, a photograph of herself on the other side."

and she was sure she would avoid the 'flyer that goes in the bin' syndrome of so many start-ups. It worked, and soon people were giving her a try for all sorts of different events. That worked too as they came back to her again and again. Word of mouth did the rest.

These one-off occasions filled summer 2019, and she was full tilt at Loyton that winter. The following summer would be filled again with the individual events that gave her work welcome change and

"The following summer would be filled again with the individual events that gave her work welcome change and variety."

variety and she'd need a trailer to make the operation really slick. That was what winning the Pinnacle Award would help towards. Then, of course, it all ground to a shuddering halt.

Caroline had been in business long enough to get some, though not all, of the support available to self-employed people. She'd paid for the equipment and fridges she needed already, and cancelled meals don't need any food bought. She had somewhere to live, with an understanding family landlord. She could manage, and she had a lot of thinking time.

We all know it's been stop start since then, with too many false dawns. But Caroline's there and ready, with new ideas to put into practice – something too about exploring opportunities for spontaneity in a time when booking ahead seems to be de rigeur. The prize money for the trailer hasn't been spent so far, the time isn't right just yet, and trailer prices are scandalously high at the moment. Caroline is poised, ready, and justly confident both of her cooking and of her business as it begins to fly again. ◆

A Withycombe

THE YEAR IN RETROSPECT

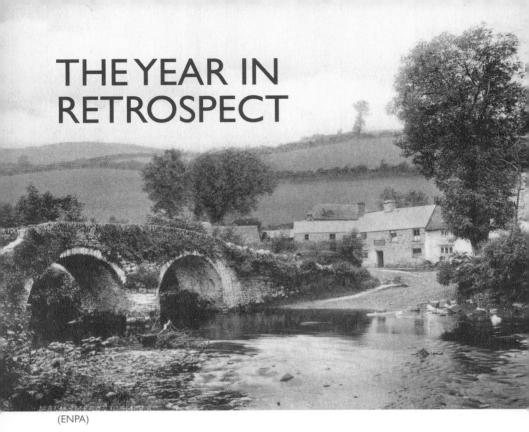

(ENPA)

The Year in Retrospect highlights the significant contributions and activities the Society has undertaken in order to achieve its charitable objective of promoting the conservation and protection of Exmoor National Park for the benefit of all.

CONSERVING & CAMPAIGNING

- Natural Capital: We continue to campaign for a record of natural capital as defined in our Register. The Society's Vice Chairman contributed to Natural England's Landscape Network webinars in December, leading on the theme: "Landscape and Natural Capital in a National Park – The Case of Exmoor. (See Spring Newsletter 2021).

- Nature Recovery: The Society was invited to take part in a Visioning exercise on the current state of nature on Exmoor. In partnership with others, nature recovery will continue to be an important aspect of our work.

- Nocturnal Exmoor: The theme of our four webinars showed the significance of darkness to wildlife and people. The webinars brought together biologists, ecologists, farmers, writers, film makers, astronomers and tourism providers to argue how much we should value darkness and its importance to different species. They are available via our website

Game Shooting Update: In 2018 the Vice Chairman was asked to look into shooting on Exmoor as the ENPA reported increased discussion about the impact of game shoots, the size and number of which have grown significantly on Exmoor over the last 20 years. Concerns were raised ranging from the relatively minor to those with discernible impacts. The report is available on our website.

The Society continues to monitor the report's recommendations but in 2021 is concerned that so far actions have been limited. Complaints continue and apply particularly to two localities. Since 2018, the context for game shooting in Exmoor has changed with new national policies for agriculture and the environment and the consequences of Covid-19. As a result, there will be more questions about game shooting in relation to its positive and negative impacts on ecology, economy, society and culture. The Society will continue to reflect on these developments and contribute to the discussion on its website.

Research Projects: The Society commissioned two projects; the first a scoping paper on Exmoor's Farming Heritage, the second to consider *Art in Support of Improved Understanding of the Changing Character of the Exmoor National Park*. The focus will be how art images, spanning the period from the 1770s to the present day, can be used to understand change.

Enjoying Exmoor: The Society welcomes people to Exmoor to enjoy its special qualities. Exmoor receives a small number of visitors compared with England's other national parks: 2 million day visits a year compared with the the smaller New Forest which receives 13 million. The pandemic led to greater numbers with overcrowding in popular places, litter and problems of overnight camping. We believe that visitor management needs to be addressed, particularly in sensitive conservation areas with no infrastructure. We are working to identify vulnerable sites and the issues raised, suggesting simple solutions and exploring the possibility of trialling more radical ones.

'Lynmouth from the Quay' by W. Spreat c.1840. Lithograph. Private Collection

Riscombe Valley (Clover Godsal)

PLANNING

The Society monitors the weekly list of new planning applications. Occasionally, the Society raises concerns and sometimes outright objection taking notice of the planning officers' recommendations.

- A retrospective proposal for change of use of an area from pasture to a timber storage area was objected to by the Society and strongly opposed by the planning officers for reasons including landscape impact and the site's location open countryside. It was similar to an application for the same site turned down two years ago but with a few additional landscaping proposals. There was strong support from the farming community for the business to continue and Authority members decided to approve the application.

- The Society objected to a proposal for an agricultural building on a small holding of ten acres in a hamlet, the Authority members decided to refuse permission. Again, a similar application for the site has been submitted.

- The Society continues to raise concerns over countryside clutter including the increase in signs, seats and fences in different sensitive landscapes and even in some settlements.

- A Planning White Paper, to which the Society responded, caused much controversy nationally and we now await the publication of the Planning Bill.

EVENTS & OUTREACH

- The annual Spring Conference in partnership with Exmoor National Park Authority (ENPA) was cancelled in 2020 and in May live webinars were held in place of the 2021 Conference. These were well received and will be used in future to complement the annual conference.

- Education: no activity for the last two years due to Covid-19.

- Walks. The Society provided an extensive walks programme led by knowledgeable guides, in different locations and on diverse themes. Covid-19 regulations originally limited numbers to six people, then thirty and finally no restrictions. The pre-booking system proved particularly popular with people who have just moved to Exmoor.

- The Resource Centre had to restrict access for much of the last year but dealt with many email queries. Work continued entering material from the estate of Victor Bonham Carter into the archive catalogue.

Donations of material have been received. (See further detail in the Spring News Letter 2021)

AWARDS & COMPETITIONS

This year's winners are as follows:

- Founder's Award – Dr Sean Beer for his support over many years and the enormous task of updating of the index catalogue of the *Exmoor Review*

- Brian & Mary Chugg Conservation Award – Linda Blanchard for her voluntary conservation work on Exmoor's heritage

- Adult Poetry Competition – Dora Allan for her poem *Wolf Moon over Exmoor*

- Lucy Perry Competition – not held

- Pinnacle Award 2020 – Caroline Westcott for her catering business

- MacEwen Essay Competition – Nick Hosegood, *Exmoor's Future Woodland.*

Enjoying Exmoor – Valley of Rocks (ENPA)

EXMOOR SOCIETY GOVERNANCE 2021

FINANCE

Total incoming resources for 2021
amount to £133,364.

The income on the general fund of
£48,143 is close to expectations apart
from shop income which was lower than
hoped due to the pandemic restrictions.

The restricted/designated fund income
of £85,221 is mainly from bequests.

Total resources expended amount to
£70,073. General fund expenditure has
been well controlled, and after transfers
resulted in a surplus of £335.

Expenditure on restricted/designated
funds totalled £17,618 and this has
mainly been spent on the completion of
the book, grants – in particular Pinnacle
Award and continuing to employ a part
time Development Co-ordinator.

The valuation of investments has
increased this year by £41,480, which
increases the net movement of funds on
the general fund to £41,815.

TRUSTEES: (EXECUTIVE)

Trustees continue the overall strategic
aims of Campaign, Conserve and Engage.
With much greater understanding of the
crises in biodiversity and climate change
the Society is emphasising action on
Nature Recovery and Climate Resilience
and Adaptation. It has offered financial
support to bodies that help achieve our
charitable aims. We have employed a
Development Coordinator to increase
the use of social media, both individual
and family membership, and corporate
sponsorship and marketing.

Despite having to deal with the
pandemic in 2020-2021 there have been
opportunities to update our policies,
public relations, and website and meet
virtually at six Trustees and six Policy
meetings and with others, particularly
the National Park Authority.

We continue to search for an honorary
Treasurer, following the remarkable
achievements of our present one, Karen
Trigger FCA who wishes to step down
in September.

CONTRIBUTOR BIOGRAPHIES

Annabel Barber
Annabel is the editor of the Blue Guides and lives in Hungary and Venn.

Dr Sean Beer
Senior academic at Bournemouth University. Sean trained as an agricultural scientist and is a Nuffield Scholar, Winston Churchill Fellow and a Rotary Foundation Scholar.

Dr Elizabeth Bradshaw
Elizabeth has lived and worked on Exmoor for over 20 years. She is a director of jh ecology ltd and a member of Somerset Bat Group.

Sarah Bryan
Chief Executive of the ENPA, with over 25 years' service. With degrees in Environmental Science (UEA) and Landscape Design (Manchester) Sarah is a Chartered Member of the Landscape Institute.

Tim Dee
Tim is a former BBC radio producer. He is the author of *The Running Sky* and *Greenery* among other books. He lives (for some of the year) in Bristol; his parents lived for several years in Minehead, allowing him many early morning excursions to Exmoor's oaks.

Jonathan Delafield Cook
Jonathan is an artist who lives near Tiverton and works from nature in charcoal.

Charles Foster
Charles is the author of many books, including *Being a Beast, The Screaming Sky,* and *Being a Human.*

Clover Godsal
Clover grew up in London and Withypool. She read Arabic and Middle Eastern studies at Cambridge and studied at the College of Fine Art in Cairo, Egypt. She now works for the FCDO and paints.

Kate Green
Deputy Editor of *Country Life*, Kate was born on Exmoor.

Nigel Hester
Nigel moved to Exmoor in 1987 and, until retirement in 2018, worked for the National Trust in countryside management and natural river and coast projects, based at the Holnicote Estate.

Dr Keith Howe
Vice-chairman, the Exmoor Society. Senior Research Fellow, Centre for Rural Policy Research, Exeter University. Award for Excellence, Agricultural Economics Society. Honorary Doctor of Veterinary Medicine, Royal Veterinary College.

Rachel Johnson
Rachel is a journalist who lives outside Winsford.

Mark Luytens,
Mark is a Landscape Designer who lives in the Barle Valley.

(© Laurence Liddy)

Georgina Macmillan
Brought up at Willingford, Georgina is studying for her BA in Photography at the University of the West of England.

George Macpherson
George is an author, publisher and Consultant Editor to *Appropriate Technology* magazine

Graeme McVittie
Has been involved in forestry and woodland management since 1977 and worked for ENPA since 1998 now as Senior Conservation Officer – Woodlands.

Fiona Mathews
Professor of Environmental Biology at the University of Sussex, Chair of the Mammal Society and a Natural Environment Research Council knowledge exchange Fellow.

Robin Milton
An Exmoor farmer passionate about the value of hill farming, ARAgS, Chairman ENPA (SoS appointee), former Chairman NFU National Hill and Upland Farming Forum, Devon Local Nature Partnership board member, Devon Farm Business Farming Champion 2018.

Kate O'Sullivan
Kate is editor of the *Exmoor Review*.

Siân Parry
Fungi Recorder for Exmoor Natural History Society.

Rachel Thomas
Chairman of the Exmoor Society, with long experience in countryside matters and rural affairs. A former geography lecturer, Countryside Commissioner, ENPA member and more. Rachel's work has been recognised with a CBE and an honorary doctorate. She is a Deputy Lieutenant of Devon.

Giles Quarme
An architect specialising in the restoration of historic buildings Giles has worked on projects including country houses, national museums and the Princess Diana Memorial Museum at Althorp.

John Wibberley
Professor of Comparative Agriculture and Rural Extension, University of Reading and Royal Agricultural University Cirencester, Exmoor Society Trustee and former Secretary of State Appointee to ENPA.

Rob Wilson-North
Rob is head of Conservation & Access for the ENPA. He previously worked with the Royal Commission on the Historical Monuments of England as a field investigator.

A Withycombe
A Withycombe has lived and worked on the edge of Exmoor for over thirty years.

With thanks to:
Lisa Eden, Laurie Greenall, Lorraine Inglis, Miranda Johnston, Anne Parham, Liz Pile, Steven Pugsley, Kayleigh Pullinger, Nicola Shane, Esme Weil, Christina Williams and Laura Yiend.

Opinions expressed in the *Exmoor Review* are not necessarily endorsed by the Exmoor Society nor by the *Exmoor Review*'s editor.

Cover picture: Red Deer Stag at Exehead, © Jochen Langbein

Volume no 63 ISBN 978 0 86183 459 4

© The Exmoor Society

Produced for the Exmoor Society by Halsgrove, Wellington, Somerset

Printed by the Short Run Press, Exeter

Cretaegus, etching on hawthorn leaves (Buckmaster&French, Arborealists)